MANIA

MY JOURNEY TO A WOMEN'S FEDERAL PRISON

BY

JANIE RENEE COCHRAN

Printed in the United States of America
First Printing June 2019

For information: Righter's Mill Press LLC
475 Wall Street
Princeton, NJ 08540

Library of Congress Cataloging-in-Publication Data
Cochran, Janie Renee
MANIA/ Janie Renee Cochran 5-3-1954

ISBN: 978-1-948460-02-6

First Edition

Jacket Designed by Brian Hailes

Visit our Web Site at:
http://www.rightersmill.com

I want to thank my beautiful daughter, Micah Jane Cochran, for her help in writing this book. Her wit and skills are displayed throughout. And without her encouragement, this book may have never been completed.

A special thanks to Dr. Joe Montes for editing my manuscript and for his encouragement.

Dedicated to the many therapists of my beloved children, Joshua, Micah, and Bryson, without whom they might not be the resilient and mostly normal adults they are today.

I love you, kids, and I am proud to be your mother.

PREFACE

I'VE DONE THINGS I'M not proud of. And I cannot and will not blame alone my mental illness for all of my bad decisions and behavior. Of course, mental illness played a huge part in my past, but at the end of day, I was at least partially responsible for what I did. I am quite aware, in any case, that I have been judged severely for at least some of these actions.

There have been victims of my past, and I hope that they will forgive me. I will not further anger these victims by telling them, "The devil made me do it," or "I didn't know what I was doing." I just want to tell all those I've wronged that I'm sorry. I do hope, nonetheless, that this book will bring some understanding to them of why things unfolded as they did.

This book will tell my story starting in my early 20s with the onset of my mental illness. Finally, I got medication which, as you will see, can be good and bad. When I first was medicated it helped, but then my life took a terrible turn. For me, the science had gone horribly wrong. This led to mania, led to crime, led to prison.

Most people I met in prison told me they were innocent, or their lawyer screwed them, or the people or institutions had it coming. By the time I made it there, I had made peace with my actions, my mental illness, and the court system. I told everyone there I was in prison because I broke the law because I was greedy. That was the superficial truth. What I didn't tell them was that my mental illness at the time contributed to those awful actions. But I cannot stress enough, at the end of the day, that the bad decisions were mine, and that I didn't feel the court system got it completely wrong by putting me away; perhaps more leniency should have been displayed considering my illness, but laws do have to be upheld.

So, as you can see, I was incarcerated. I know, I know, people go to prison every single day. So what? Why am I interesting? I am interesting because I am your mother, your sister, your friend, your colleague; hell… I could even be YOU! The story you are about to read is as real as I could reconstruct it; the dialogue is as faithful as a re-creation will permit. Although it is not a work of fiction, I don't know a single person who could, verbatim, recall every single word and inflection of voice in a conversation. Thus, the therapeutic sessions recounted here actually took longer than they will appear in this book, as should be obvious. I was much too tough a cookie to crack in just a few pointed quips from a doctor. Nonetheless, I have kept to the spirit and substance of all that transpired. Of course, except in the case of close friends and family members, I have changed the names of some of the characters in the story to protect their privacy.

While what happened to me is sad, it helps to tell a story of how easy it is to fall from grace, and how our culture isn't necessarily built to catch and rehabilitate us after that fall, much less prevent it. Now the mother of three grown children, two boys and a girl, I continue to find myself in a predicament that bears witness to the flawed nature of all of us. On the one hand, any of us can make mistakes we will later regret and have to account for. Our justice system does not usually allow for an understanding of mental illness and seems to pretend that only good and evil exist, but not mental health and drug addiction.

I hope this story intrigues you, and in the process, sheds light on the condition of all of us as people, and on the condition of our system of justice, itself the creation of people, who after all, as we already know, are flawed, too. From the start, I want to state that my story is not about falling down. It's about getting back up again when all you really want to do is just give up and pull the covers up over your head and say, "Screw it!"

CHAPTER 1

IT WAS MAY 1994. I was standing outside. The smell of spring. Just an hour before, I watched my three school-aged children get on the big yellow bus, singing the "no more pencils, no more books, no more teachers' dirty looks" song as the end of the school year loomed. The upper-middle-class neighborhood I had spent 10 years living in boasted manicured lawns and the gloss of morning grass, still wet from so many sprinklers. I waved hello to my neighbor across the street, Nancy; she gave me a forced half-smile and low-waisted wave, you know, the kind of wave you give someone when you don't want the rest of the world seeing you acknowledge someone. Maybe Nancy and her husband Jim were having trouble again; maybe she was jealous of my very active social life and handsome boyfriends, or maybe she was just uncomfortable seeing me in my pink nightie. What, a woman can't stand on her lawn wearing anything but her best Victoria's Secret? Whatever...

This particular morning was sunny and promised to become a beautiful day. I had just begun making plans when I found myself sitting in the back of a sedan, handcuffed, with two federal marshals beside me. Now, in my defense, I would have gotten dressed, but the officers forbade me from re-entering my house. I was dazed and confused. In all of my life, I had never seen someone arrested in front of me, much less been the one in handcuffs. A seasoned moviegoer, I knew they had to read me my rights and give me phone calls, but one thing I didn't prepare for, was the Egg McMuffin. That's right, these generous officers while arresting me in my underwear for thirteen felony counts, made sure that I got an Egg McMuffin for breakfast. Sitting in the McDonald's parking lot, I okayed around and saw commuters coming and going to work, and here I was trying to cover my nipples, figure out how to eat while handcuffed, and make sense of what was happening while the federal marshals were happily eating their breakfasts.

Let me back up a little. It all started at around 8:00 am. My kids had just gotten on the bus and were headed for school. Thank God they missed the drama. I was leaving my house to give my nephew a ride to work and was surprised by two sedans flying into my driveway. Four federal marshals quickly emerged and approached, announcing, "This is the day," and ordered me to put my hands behind my back. Oh, I knew what day they were referring to alright. This day had been long in coming.

I put my hands behind my back as instructed, was handcuffed, and placed in one of the sedans. We drove to the local McDonald's and met up with two more sedans and four more marshals. It amazed me that the feds had sent six marshals to arrest me. They knew I would have no weapons and that in actuality I was only a housewife and minor league immigration fraud boss. But be that as it was, they sent six agents. Looking back, I feel a little sorry for them; someone must've thought they'd find Jimmy Hoffa's body or cases of cocaine buried under my kids' swing set.

I was startled when the car's back door opened and one of the federal marshals instructed me to get out. I did as I was told and stepped into the parking lot. Customers entering the McDonald's stared at me standing there surrounded by six people while I was in that damned nightie with my hands handcuffed behind me. Then it hit me: the feds were putting me on display, essentially trying to embarrass me in front of my community. Think 18th-century witch trials, or the book

The Scarlet Letter. But instead of itchy bonnets and heavy-wool dresses, we have sheer nighties and McDonald's parking lots. Well, the joke is on them. I had already been humiliated in *The Washington Post, The Baltimore Sun*, and my local newspaper. Standing in my nightie in the parking lot of McDonald's was child's play to me.

Once again, I was instructed to sit in the back of a sedan, a different one this time. One of the marshals must have remembered something more important than his McMuffin and turned around and read me my rights. He asked me if I understood, and I pointed out that he had cheese on his upper lip.

I understood my rights. After all, the movies we watch played them out over and over; and what I did not learn from the cinema, my attorney had reinforced many times. I knew I had the right to remain silent, the advice I should have taken a year earlier, but instead, I chose the right to make a fool out of myself. I also knew I had the right to an attorney, and if I couldn't afford one, one would be appointed for me. Yes, I got it, got it all. At least the one marshal had been kind enough to take off the handcuffs so I could eat that damned Egg McMuffin. I had no idea when I would eat again.

I was driven to a sixteen-story professional building in the city of Baltimore. As I rode the elevator to the booking area, workers were staring me up and down. I'm sure I was a sight standing there, and by this time, I was shivering. It was cold and not one marshal seemed to take notice that I was practically convulsing. People were coming and going, all wearing professional attire. And when they saw me half naked and shaking, they quickly looked away. At least some people had manners.

This was the day, the day I had waited for over a year, the day I was arrested for immigration fraud. It was the day I would have to make bail, and despite my year of warnings, I had no one in mind who could post bail for me. Maybe this professional building was going to become my home until trial. I just wasn't sure.

CHAPTER 2

I WAS BORN IN 1954, in a small town in Illinois across the Mississippi from St. Louis, Missouri. I would describe my upbringing as middle class, surface-level Norman Rockwell per my mother's tireless efforts. My brother, Terry, was four years older than I and every bit the tyrant older brothers usually are. My mother, Betty, stayed home and raised Terry and me, and my dad, Odell, worked at the time as a lineman on the poles, as many of the other fathers did in our circle of friends. Ever the go-getter, my father graduated to union manager and eventually got transferred to Washington, D.C. We bought a home in Maryland where I had my first dances with psychotic episodes, mental illness, drugs, marriage, and children, in no particular order.

My parents, through my childhood, took my brother and me to a Baptist church, and for the most part, my mom and dad were easygoing, that is if you choose to overlook my mother's narcissism. To this day, and despite having a clinician for a daughter, it's impossible to know where my mother's narcissistic and controlling nature stems from. She herself had great and loving parents but was very poor and grew up in the middle of an army of children. My dad, who had a violent father, was so calm I sometimes wondered if he wasn't a saint. He had a wickedly funny sense of humor. My mother was funny in her own right as well, mostly when she was telling you like it was.

5

I remember once waking up shortly after having fallen asleep one evening, hearing music coming from the living room. I got out of bed and crept into the living room where I saw my mom and dad sitting on the couch listening to Conway Twitty singing one of his famous songs, "It's Only Make Believe". I walked in and my dad stood up. Instead of shooing me back to bed, he grabbed my hand, placed my small feet on his, and we danced. I was a marionette doll, in bliss. It was magical. I know it sounds like something you see on *Hallmark* or in country music videos, but this was my dad. On that occasion, my mother looked upon her husband and daughter with rarely seen gentility and pride.

I can recall as a teenager going to some of my wealthier friends' homes and then returning to our smaller house complaining about not having what so and so had. One evening I came home and complained that one of my friends had a color TV in her bedroom! My dad walked over to the refrigerator and pulled out a carton of ice cream. He scooped some into my bowl and then some into his. He sat down across from me. "But do they have delicious ice cream as we have?" I was furious. "They have friggin' color TV's in their rooms and dishwashers in their kitchens. I'm sure they have ice cream." He looked at me, shrugged, and with a small wink replied, "But theirs probably isn't as good as ours."

Years later I realized that most of my wealthier friends envied me. I had a mother and father who loved one another. I had a father everyone adored, who sat with his daughter eating delicious ice cream. It turns out my dad was right. Theirs was not as delicious as ours.

But I still wonder to this day, and I've asked my therapists if my anxiety stemmed from the control my mother had over me and our family. If my mother disapproved of our actions, she would shun us until we came around to her way of seeing things. She did this to me as an adult as well. I do believe this contributed to my high levels of anxiety and the desperate need to be approved at any cost. My mother could go for years upon years not talking to someone just because she felt betrayed on some matter. No one wanted to cross her; we all sought her approval. I no longer need to ask a therapist if this contributed to my anxiety. I now know it did. I also know about conditional and unconditional love. I received unconditional love from my father. I received conditional love from my mother. My father taught me self-worth, and that in turn made me feel powerful. My mother taught me that if you make people mad or angry, they, in turn, will cut you out of their life. She set that example from the time I was a child.

When I was young, we were never alone. I had tons of cousins. We would frequently drive three hours to Missouri to visit them every other weekend and all summer. Family was all around me, and that's why I wanted one of my own. I wanted children, cousins for them to play and grow up with, and a nice home in the suburbs.

In school, I was definitely an underachiever. I was happy just passing a course. My parents never pressed me to do better. Looking back, I think I suffered from depression but never was formally diagnosed. My problem was that I would daydream for hours while in class. When the bell rang, it jolted me; I was 1,000 miles away in a daydream. Some of my teachers spoke to my parents about it, but back in the 50s and 60s, everyone thought things like that were only a phase, that I would grow out of it. Some parents believed in beating a child into doing better, but my parents were more like the "go-at-your-own-pace type." Maybe that was good, maybe that was bad, but that's the way things were. When I graduated from high school, I don't think I even knew how to string an intelligent sentence together. I was doing eighth-grade math and knew very little about the world I lived in. But I had street smarts, and I guess that's what saved my ass.

Growing up in the 60s, I remember only too well the discrimination that was all around me. I was just a child when at the St. Louis

Zoo I read a sign above a water fountain that read, "Whites Only." I asked my dad why it mattered, and he replied, "To some, it does, but don't pay any attention to it." At that young age, I had the privilege of blissful ignorance. If you would have told me then as a child, later as a teenager, or even later as a young adult that I would be discriminated against later in my life I would have laughed. Preposterous.

All through elementary school up to the 4th grade, my class was all white. In 4th grade, the school had its first black student, a girl named Nancy. I remember the teacher making an announcement to the class that someone of "color," a "Negro," was going to be joining us in our classroom and we were not to stare at her. Well, once she said not to stare, it was all I could do. When Nancy came into class, she sat one row behind me. I kept dropping my pencil on the ground so I could bend over and look at her while I picked it up. She looked so foreign. Her hair was different, her skin was different, and her clothes were different. I didn't know then, but her family was very poor, and they sent Nancy to school in her older siblings' hand-me-downs that were five sizes too big.

I don't know to this day what happened to Nancy, but I do know that the little girl that joined us in the 4th grade that day had more guts than I'll ever have. She walked into a classroom filled with white kids, kids with parents who probably looked down on her and her parents, and even though she was surrounded by strangers she had grace and courage. Later, when I was alone with my thoughts in prison, I would think about Nancy and what became of her. Now, I was the one who was different….

As I emerged into my teenage years, I had the usual array of boy-friends. Throughout high school, I went to all the usual dances and parties, though I didn't really push the envelope with teenage high jinx until after I graduated. If I even got close to a boy's penis, I feared pregnancy. I might fool around with a boy, but never, never would "go all the way", because I knew I would have been ostracized by my family if they ever found out; my mother had made that quite clear. But after high school, that was different, that's when I discovered the pill. Oh, the pill! Just swallow a little pink pill, and you could dance with that sexy devil all you wanted and not fear the "off-with-your-head" speech from your mother and the ball-and-chain of unplanned motherhood.

The pill opened up many new doors for girls back then. Finally, a woman could have sex without worrying about getting pregnant, like men had been doing for years. I think I found equal footing with boys back then. I no longer had to fear pregnancy; I was free to experiment. But that did go directly against my Baptist upbringing, hard to settle in my mind. But I compromised; I was a Baptist Monday through Thursday, a young woman on the pill Friday through Sunday.

I had no real aspirations after high school other than to get married and have children. My brother followed our father into electrical work, and I guess I was following my mother into domestic life. After I graduated from high school, my dad landed me a job with a union in Washington, D.C. where I worked as a secretary for a lobbyist. I just could have been the worst secretary on the planet. No, on second thought, I am sure I was the worst secretary on Earth. The only thing that kept me from being fired was my sense of humor and a modicum of charm. If one of the lobbyists asked for a letter to be typed—and this was before computers—it took me hours. I would misspell every other word and get distracted by others in office gossip. I was terrible. But I was skilled in small talk and fetching coffee for everyone—and I was cute. But it didn't actually bother me that I was terrible because all I ever really wanted to be was a wife and a mother. I used to watch the clock at work and daydream about being in my own home and decorating it. I saw myself greet the kids after school and prepare dinner. Female coworkers made fun of me, which I didn't mind, as they had different ambitions in life. I just wanted to be Suzie Homemaker. But first I had to get some partying years behind me. And suddenly it all came to a screeching halt while I was listening to the Steve Miller Band.

It was 1973. The Steve Miller song, "Keep on Rocking Me Baby," was blasting on the radio. I had four friends crammed in my Dodge, and my speedometer was broken. It was stuck on 100 miles per hour. I would drive around with my friends, and as they got high or drunk, they would suddenly look at the speedometer and freak out. I was probably going 40 miles per hour, but they would think I was doing 100. Funny how they took issue with my speeding, but never minded the intravenous drugs and french fries shared in my backseat.

One night I was driving around, nowhere in particular; we never went anywhere in particular. Just drove around our community like the idiots we were, wasting precious fuel. Back then it took me all of five dollars to fill up my tank. We would all chip in a buck here and there, and then off into the night we would go. And did we worry about DWI's? Not a bit. I remember being pulled over a couple of times by a policeman for speeding while I was totally drunk and high, and the officer just telling me to go home, or sometimes even offering me or my friends a ride. A far cry from today, but honestly, I believe the laws we have today about drinking and driving are better than those of the good old days. Too many of us either got killed while drinking and driving or we killed someone else.

As the Steve Miller song played, I took a hit of weed. Suddenly, I was overwhelmed with terror and paranoia. I had smoked pot before, but this time, a gut-wrenching fear gripped me, and I began to hyper-ventilate. Normally, you can identify a trigger for your fear, like a spider, and remove the stimulus. But I couldn't do that. I couldn't keep a rational or straight thought in my head. From the tips of my toes to the center of my churning gut, all I could make sense of was doom. I managed to park the car somewhere. I dashed out. When the terror subsided, I was still confused and frightened. Or as they say today, "dazed and confused." One of the stoners fell out of the car and asked me what the hell was going on. I just doubled over and told him I didn't know.

"Bad trip, eh?" he asked with his eyes fighting to stay open and his body hunched halfway outside of the car.

"Yeah," I said. "Bad fucking trip." I got back in the car and asked everyone if the pot was laced with anything. The one who brought it said it wasn't; it was the same batch they had all smoked for weeks.

I stared at him. "Well, what in the actual fuck just happened?

"You probably had a panic attack," he said. "That's a common reaction to pot."

"How in the hell do you know what I just felt? Are you a psychiatrist? Common? I never heard that before."

He replied, "I read about it somewhere, and it happens to my sister a lot. That's why she switched to just drinking wine. She can't handle pot anymore."

"You think?" I said with a laugh.

Whatever it was, it was intense. I was freaking out. Freaking out! Out-of-mind experience. It felt like my back was up against a brick wall, nowhere to turn or run to, a wild tiger staring me down and charging me. My brain froze; I was in a state of terror; I was losing my mind.

"Kind of ruined the whole Steve Miller experience, didn't it?" the guy said, laughing.

"Oh, fuck you. I'm being serious."

"So am I."

I wrote it off as a bad pot experience and went on with my life. But weeks after that first panic attack, I had another one. This time I wasn't smoking pot. I was walking down K Street in D.C., going to meet my carpool. The same terror seized me, and I froze in my tracks. I felt like I was going to hyperventilate, and when the symptoms subsided, I was shaking. From then on, the panic attacks started coming at me like waves crashing onto the shores of my life. They came with no rhyme, warning, or reason. I didn't know when to expect them. I didn't know what triggered them. I became a prisoner. I was going crazy. Who could I tell? Who would understand? Up until the cute stoner with the wino sister, I had never even heard of a panic attack. My friends would surely think I'm a lunatic and not want to hang around me; my family would make me feel like I disgraced them for having some mental experiences that they couldn't fit into their pretty box. Most importantly, I was afraid of what was brewing inside of me. Therefore, I did the only reasonable thing a girl could do: I swept it under the rug and tried to ignore it.

But they came, they still came, and when they did, I would feel extreme, intense terror. As soon as the terror crested, it would begin to descend back into normalcy, leaving me feeling that my surroundings were surreal. My palms were sweaty after each attack, and it took hours to feel stable. What the hell was happening? There was terror in my mind, and it was made worse by the fear of yet another attack. Anxiety times 1,000!

I began to stay indoors for fear I would have another attack and lose control in public. I developed what psychiatrists call 'agoraphobia', irrational fear of open areas, outdoors especially. I didn't, or felt I couldn't, leave my home. I couldn't go anywhere. I couldn't escape from that fear that I would have another panic attack. My biggest fear was that I would have an attack in public and be out of control. It was irrational thinking on my part—or was it? I imagined that I would leave home, go to a public place, have a terrorizing attack, lose control, and they would have to lock me up somewhere where I would have even less control.

Agoraphobia kidnapped my social life. There was no more hanging out with friends or going to the mall or trips to get groceries. It's all about staying in your own environment, home, where you feel safe. It's hard for me to explain why your mind goes there. It's more of a fear of having panic attacks in an open area and having nowhere to run and hide. Keep in mind we are talking about an era when most mental health treatments for acute level conditions involved restraints, rubber rooms, and electric shock therapy. No thank you. Fear of the unknown left me inside my home for many weeks at a time. Since I had a job, I had to make decisions about how I was going to address my agoraphobia.

If I could have, I probably would have stayed home indefinitely, maybe forever, and never gone past my front door. But since I was in my 20s and living at home, I knew my mother would be in my face about not working and who was going to support me. My mother was a believer in "pull yourself up by your bootstraps," and this time I had to take her advice. Faced with having to choose between the lesser of two evils, somehow, I had to reach down inside and find the strength to walk out that door into the open and face what was to come. I took all my vacation time at my job, which was two weeks, and stayed inside. I thought by doing so I would eventually work up the courage to go outside. I made small strides at first, such as walking outside to the street. When I did that, I felt encouraged since I had finally gone outside and didn't fall apart.

The Saturday afternoon before I went back to work, a friend came by and wanted to know if I wanted to go to her house and look at her vacation slides. I felt as if I had just been asked to jump out of an airplane without a parachute. I knew I had to go back to work that Monday, so I swallowed hard and mustered up the courage to go. That friend of mine, like the others, had no idea what was going on inside my head. She, like most, just thought I was being unsociable and going through a phase. No one knew the terror that was in my mind because of the paralyzing fear of another panic attack, of losing control. It was indescribable.

I was almost shaking when I got in her car. I remember distinctly her talking, and when we got to the end of my street and she was about to turn left, I was flooded with anxiety and with the thought, there is no turning back, what will be will be. And then I began to think some comforting thoughts, like, so what if I have a huge panic attack in front of her, so what? Then at least she will know I'm suffering. and maybe I'll get some help.

Am I out of control? What was I going to do, jump out of her car while she was driving? Again, so what? Then at least people will see the depths of my pain and maybe this will bring me help. My final thought, while we were driving, was, I don't give a crap anymore. I'm tired of being held hostage by my irrational thoughts. Go ahead, Janie, lose control. Let the world see the anguish that you are in. In fact, I hoped I would lose control. Let the world see. Oh, how I wish I could have just talked to her about it, without having to go through every worst-case scenario in my head.

And you know what happened? Nothing. I felt calm and collected when I got to my friend's house. I felt a silent sense of pride for making it through another small step, the car ride, that long, terrifying car ride, without slipping into the abyss. The satisfaction and relief I felt fueled me to keep moving. I looked at her vacation pictures and, while I would like to say I stayed there all afternoon, that would not be true. I did get antsy and wanted to go to my protective home, but I stayed long enough to see her slides and not have an episode. I made a huge stride.

I went to work the next day, and the day after that, and the day after that. I had some setbacks, panic attacks at work, but it didn't lead to staying indoors as before. Nevertheless, I lived in fear; all was not perfect, but at least my thoughts weren't holding me captive in my home. And what helped the most? The "I don't care anymore attitude." Just go and get it over with, that is, getting out of control and losing it. I was tired and just wanted to live a normal life. Once I faced my fears, they all but disappeared. I am not saying that it's just that easy to conquer agoraphobia. I'm just saying that for me it really helped to call the monster out of the closet and tell him to go fuck himself. He could hold me, hostage, no more.

To be honest that's not the whole story. I left out a huge part. I did not do this on my own. The start was mine but not the finish. Those irrational fears only went away for good when I took medication. Only then did I begin to feel normal again. Not leaving my home was never, I mean never, an issue again. And even on medication, I have setbacks, but I now know that medication can be tweaked to address my issues and that I have a chemical imbalance in my brain which leads to irrational thoughts. And finally, I no longer blame myself. A chemical imbalance is not my fault. It affects my neurotransmitter levels and my hormonal balance. I'm just as sick as someone with diabetes. It feels good to no longer blame myself and be labeled "weak" or "strange."

Thus, it makes sense to make a trip to the OBGYN and shrink before being put on meds! But before being put on medications, I did live in fear of panic attacks. I stopped socializing for fear I would have an attack. I only went to work and back home. And did I ever start screwing up at my job? I was already a terrible secretary, but now I was like a bad secretary on crack. I don't think I performed one task correctly. There was no one I could share this with. My boyfriend at the time was a big weed man, and he couldn't understand why anyone just wouldn't "fucking love pot." They had not coined the term "panic attacks" yet. I didn't even know what to call what I was experiencing. No computer to Google it, and couldn't look it up at the library since I had no idea what to search for. My boyfriend at the time started every sentence with, "Hey, man," and if I had shared it with him his response probably would have been extended to, "Hey, man, that sounds fucked up." I knew he would be useless to talk to.

As I said, my mom is the "pull-yourself-up-by-your-bootstraps" kind of person. My dad, he was sweet but had no understanding of psychiatry. He always said psychiatrists were a waste of time. I wasn't seeing many friends and didn't trust they would understand, anyway. I wasn't particularly close to any of my coworkers. I was lonely, and while becoming used to my symptoms, was nervous about how they were pervading my life.

I made an appointment with my OBGYN and told him what I was going through, thinking these panic attacks could be hormonal. In fact, it felt good to think it was hormonal, that way I could rationalize it wasn't something bad happening in my brain. I finally worked up the nerve to tell my mom that something was happening. She agreed that it was probably hormonal, pushing aside it could have anything to do with mental illness. She would say things like, "I get very emotional also when my period is off. It's probably linked to your period. You go and see him. I'm sure he'll fix you right up with hormone pills."

Well, the good doctor didn't agree with my mother. He told me after a few blood tests and a couple of visits later, that in fact it was not hormonal, and that probably I needed to see a psychiatrist. And then he threw in that he could do an exploratory operation on me to see if my female parts were in working order. I briefly considered it, and then thought no better of the idea. Something told me my vagina wasn't the culprit, and to follow a false lead would be a waste of time. It would mean being hospitalized, put to sleep, and then going through recovery time. And my inner voice kept telling me it wasn't about my ovaries at all; it was all in my brain.

It was 1974, but it might as well have been the Dark Ages. No one knew much about what was going on in the brain. I'm surprised the OBGYN didn't suggest a lobotomy. Maybe he did, I just don't remember. I got very depressed and didn't know what the hell was happening to me. I thought pot had permanently damaged me and couldn't talk to anyone about it, especially my family. And how could I tell my friends I had a bad pot experience? They wouldn't have been able to keep a straight face. And go on to tell them that the bad experience keeps continuing even when I'm not smoking weed?

"Hey, Jim, remember that pot we smoked last week?"

"Yeah," he would respond.

"Well, that was some strong shit, man! I tripped on that stuff and am still trippin' even when I'm not smoking."

"Say what?" he would say, surprised.

That's exactly how the conversation would have gone down. I did try to broach the subject with my pothead boyfriend, and his response was as predicted, "Man, I think it's all in your head."

"No shit, stupid," I said. "But exactly what is going on in my brain, you whack-out?" He didn't have an answer; he just rolled over and took another hit off his joint.

My family opposed my going to see a psychiatrist, as that was for the mentally ill, the homeless people who push around shopping carts while muttering to themselves. Certainly not for me, a person raised with a loving family and support. Going to a psychiatrist would have been a black mark on them, they certainly would have thought.

In my family, we were forbidden to use the "P" word. Not the word "pussy," but the word "psychiatrist." Psychiatrists were for the weak of character. My family was above such maladies of the mind. If I had to see a psychiatrist, my parents would have to either deduce they were bad parents and raised me poorly, or that my malady was genetic. Either way, it would be a lose-lose situation for them. So, the answer to that was, if I go to a psychiatrist, make it like the now-antiquated view of homosexuals in the military during the Clinton years: "Don't ask, don't tell."

But I will admit it was a deflating moment for me once I decided I had to seek professional help. Psychiatrists were the bad guys. The scary guys. It was though I had decided to see a witch doctor, crazy headpieces, white face paint, straw amulets, chanting. All I knew of psychiatrists was what I saw on TV or in movies. The last time I saw a psychiatrist in a movie was "The Three Faces of Eve," with Joanne

Woodward. Then I got to thinking. Did I have multiple personalities? How crazy was I? My mind raced from one strange thing to the next.

And to make matters worse, *One Flew over the Cuckoo's Nest* had just been released. Jack Nicholson in a mental hospital with assorted loons. My pothead boyfriend dragged me out of the house to see it, and all through that movie, I kept envisioning myself living in that insane asylum. I almost wished a big, tall Native American would smother me. Worse, would I end up with a lobotomy? When I got home, I jumped into bed and pulled the covers up over my head.

This was my life in the 70s. Hiding in my house, fighting off panic attacks and dreading the next one. I tried to appear normal and let no one know what was going on because in essence, I myself didn't know. I had been taught all my life that being seen as normal and happy was what my mother expected. I did my best not to let her down.

Through all this, I didn't pray much and didn't feel particularly close to God. You could say I felt somewhat betrayed by God. Why would He allow an illness to invade my brain? And even worse, without some sort of treatment being available? But God did give me something. He gave me a friend that I met apparently quite by accident. She, too, was suffering from the same mental illness I was. We became close friends and would talk for hours. I felt vindicated when I spoke to her and knew then I wasn't alone. This is partly why I'm writing this book. I never want another person to feel alone with this illness.

CHAPTER 3

YEARS WENT BY AFTER my first panic attack, and yes, I did see a few psychiatrists. One in particular, in the early 80s, put me on life-saving mental medications. He made it possible for me to live without fear of a panic attack. But then, years later, I was being court-ordered to see another mental-health expert. I had just been released from prison after having been locked up for a year (for what?). It was 1996. I was assigned to a halfway house, and one of the conditions of the release was for me to see a psychologist.

I knew I would tell him my story of how I ended up in prison and my struggle with mental illness, but I was freshly released, and quite frankly didn't feel like being court ordered to do a damn thing. I spent one year and several months being told where to stand, what to eat, when to get up, and when to go to sleep. Now, I'm released, in a halfway house, but being told again what to do.

"Hi, Janie, come on in. I'm Dr. Marks. It's a pleasure to put a face to the name on the referral. Please have a seat."

Have a seat my ass, I thought. I knew why I was here. He knew why I was here, and anyone that read *The Washington Post* knew why I was here. Yes, I was court ordered.

I looked him over, a nice-looking guy, maybe fortyish, but I was betting he was younger than I. He had only spoken a few words to me at this point, so I couldn't make an assessment of his stodginess. To my dismay, he was not the homely schmoe I had hoped he would be.

"Hmm. Okay. I'll sit down, but I won't talk to you. Ask as many questions as you like. I won't answer them. They can court order me to see you, but they can't make me talk to you." I was having my *Good Will Hunting* moment. The movie was yet to be released, but I think they stole a page from my life story.

"That's right, Janie, they can't make you talk. I can't make you talk. I've been paid for a fifty-five-minute session, so let me know when you're ready. I'll just sit here and catch up on some reading."

I sat in silence for 45 minutes, watching the doctor flip through files, and curiously, he never looked over at me, not even once. The first solid ten minutes of our stalemate I sat in triumph. Ha, I didn't have to carry this guy down my yellow-brick road of shame. The next 25 minutes I was at war with reality. Even if we spent this entire session in silence, he would still document that I was disengaged. If I come in here with walls up and mouth shut every time, it could be viewed as non-compliant by my parole board. I would have to hatch another plan, one that didn't involve my doing any real work.

Suddenly, he startled me when he spoke. "Since we only have ten minutes left, I think I'll take my chances and ask you some questions."

I just shrugged my shoulders. Shoulder shrugs could be documented as a response, right?

"Why were you ordered to see me, Janie?" he asked.

I responded, "Oh, c'mon, Doc. You've got the papers right in front of you; I see my name on that file there. I'm sure they told you what it was all about. Why are you bothering to ask me?"

I didn't like what I was feeling. I was irritated and angry, and out of the confines of a prison camp or of a halfway house where I could be irritated and angry and it was simply the cultural norm. Why was I taking it out on this seemingly nice man? Because he was poking the bear? He was only trying to do his job. But I felt infringed upon, once more, by the federal government. I had done my time, all of it, now why did I have to be forced to see a shrink? And for how long would I have to see this shrink? Until the federal government decides I'm stable enough to rejoin society? I hoped that wasn't the case since that might take a lifetime.

He looked down at a file which I guess it was mine, and said, "Well, I read their side of it, but there are two sides to every story. What's your side?"

"I'll tell you my story. I got sick, took meds, committed a crime, went to prison, and lost my home, business, and pride. Now, I'm here. End of story." Damn, I was feeling so angry.

"Aw! No happy ending? You don't have a happy version for me? Geeze, quite depressing."

"Your whole job sounds depressing to me, Doc, listening to people who are screwed up and wanting answers, answers you can't give them. Well, let me clue you in on something, Doc. I'm not looking for answers from you. The only question I want an answer to is, 'Why in the hell can't an inmate take back fruit to her room without being punished?' Do you have the answer?"

"Nope, Janie, I do not."

"You don't sound like you're a very good shrink."

"Oh? What does a good shrink sound like, Janie? I'll try to find one for you."

"Typical shrink comeback," I answered. I had to force back a smile here. I friggin' love bantering.

"Well, time is up. What a boring session, don't you agree? I was expecting a somewhat more interesting story than 'I got sick, blah, blah, blah.' Maybe next time."

I grabbed my purse, walked to the door, turned around to face him, and said, "There won't be a next time."

"Oh? Aren't you forgetting the court order, Janie?"

"Oh, fuck you, Mr. Doctor with-none-of-the-answers." I left, but not without slamming the door behind me. Damn, I thought, this is just like torn out pages from *Good Will Hunting*.

When I left, I felt like kicking myself in the ass. For starters, of course, there was going to be a next time. Saying that there wouldn't be was as silly as a toddler grounding his parents. I also had to accept that he was only trying to help, but I wouldn't let him. I could feel heaviness in my chest, and I knew it was anxiety. Why wouldn't I let this man help me? I consider myself a friendly person, so why all the hostility? Of course, I knew the answer to that. I was being *forced* to do something. It didn't matter that it was for my own good. It was the point that I was tired of being told what to do. I was being oppositional, defiant. I'd already given them nearly two damn years, now this? "Give to Caesar what is Caesar's," as the Bible states. Well, I gave to Caesar my time and to the federal government my restitution. My trauma, my hurt, my disappointments, and my fears belonged to me, not Dr. Marks or anyone else.

Actually, I knew I wanted to see him again and spill out everything. The illness, the losses, the crime, sentencing, and prison. It was all inside of me waiting to come out. I had been released from prison. Wasn't that something to be happy about and to count my blessings for? Living in a halfway house wasn't as bad as living in the confines of a prison, I rationalized. I would just go back to the halfway house and wait for my next visit to Dr. Marks.

CHAPTER 4

IT WAS A BEAUTIFUL spring day in May 1996. I was walking down the streets of Washington, D.C., strolling leisurely, looking into shop windows, enjoying my new-found freedom. I could hear the birds singing, and the sun was warm against my skin. The slow-paced morning lent itself to the sense of Zen as if I were strolling these streets yoga mat in hand, fresh sweat on my brow, inner peace renewed. I was beginning to enjoy this peace when waves of paranoia broke against me. Every uniformed person, somebody in a badged uniform, even one donning a more like the "would-you-like-fries-with-that?" variety, reminded me that while I am not on the inside anymore, the outside may never feel the same as before. If you can imagine the Dalai Lama meets Red from *The Shawshank Redemption*, you might get the picture.

I caught a glimpse of myself in one of the shop windows and was happy with what I saw. I had gotten into shape in prison, and my figure at age 43 was still youthful. There are few things in the world more pleasing than being proven right, so in that shop mirror, I gave myself a little mental wink and nod. You see, upon entering what we prisoners called Camp Cupcake, I assured my friends and family that upon my release I would not come out tattooed, toothless, or affiliated with prison gangs. To the naked eye, I came out just as I entered, the token Barbie cul-de-sac mother of three. My moment of admitted self-absorption in the mirror was quickly compromised with a wince, as I remembered I had an appointment with Dr. Marks tomorrow, the court ordered psychologist. I did my best to push the thought of the pending session out of my mind. I could stroll all afternoon if I so desired, actually buy things that didn't come from the commissary, perhaps even Christmas gifts for my kids that weren't handmade from magazine scraps or old cigarette cartons.

I stopped at one of the stores and wandered inside. It was nice to go into a shop and look around without someone barking out orders like the guards inside. No one was looking over my shoulder or giving me time constraints. I opted for retail therapy this day; if you wish, call it defiance toward the inevitable *actual* therapy. But I did have to report back to the halfway house by nine pm, so in essence, I was still tied to the government. But today I didn't think about that. I simply was enjoying things that I had missed the last three years: sunshine, birds singing, and people strolling past me going about their days.

I looked at some of the people passing by and wondered what they were doing. Were they going to jobs or just shopping like I was? So many things they could be doing. In prison, I knew what everyone was doing. They were either going to their designated jobs, to the commissary or cafeteria, or back to their rooms that served as our cells. Wasn't hard to figure out since there were so few options. That was one of the biggest adjustments to being in prison. Since people-watching and nosiness had always been an Olympic sport to me, having had that taken away was cruel and unusual punishment.

Walking around the park in D.C., I started to think about the following day. I was to have another visit with Dr. Marks, and although I still felt bitter, maybe this would be the session where I unleashed my pent-up feelings. I barely began to make sense of what had become of my life since it was nearly destroyed by the love affair between mania and bad decisions. Now I was being ordered to spill my guts to some poor government-contracted schmoe who'll have a hard time making eye contact with me through the piles of manila envelopes on his desk, reminding us both that we're in over our heads.

I passed by a coffee shop and noticed some people in professional attire sipping coffee and reading newspapers. I thought back to the day when I was news in *The Washington Post*. Being famous is something every young person desires, but infamous? I never wanted that, especially for my children. Soon after my arrest, reporters began coming to my children's schools for pictures of them and hoping for statements about these "poor children's" felon mother and her entourage of exotic nannies. One night after the schools had informed me of breaches of security and what they were doing to ensure our children's privacy, a girlfriend of mine and I poured some wine and decided to play a game called "talk to the hand" with my children ages six, nine, and ten. In the game, my friend and I would try to bait the children with questions about their private home life, and they'd have to say, "Talk to the hand." The kids would lose points for making eye contact with the reporter when answering a question even vaguely or becoming upset when the reporter would harass them. When I held my two sons and my daughter in the delivery room, I had dreams of playing Patty Cake, Ring Around the Rosie, maybe even a little Hungry, Hungry, Hippos, but never did I imagine a day that I would design a game for my kids where the object was to run from people and protect their mother.

I headed back to the halfway house because I honestly didn't know what to do with myself. What started as a beautiful day of immersion back into mainstream life turned into more of that pesky self-criticism, I was being court ordered to indulge in. Damn it! In the last year-and-a-half I had so few choices, and now, today, was left with spare time, so I just couldn't think. The sun felt great on my skin, the people chatting as they passed me sounded comforting, but it was time to head back and get into my room, where once again I would feel regulated.

Maybe the regulation wouldn't be so bad for tonight, I thought, as it could help manage the emotions bubbling out that I was so desperately trying to control. There would be other days ahead of me for sunshine and strength.

I returned to the halfway house that afternoon and just flopped on the bed. I was exhausted. I thought of myself as Manny Pacquiao, the lightweight boxing champ of quips and zingers to the curious minds of the population at large. I had over 40 solid years of experience at avoiding the truth about myself, redirecting the valiant efforts made by those trying to achieve closeness to me, cushioning their fall with my charm. Admittedly, prison threw me off my game. At Camp Cupcake I didn't have to swear allegiance to white supremacists or marry big Bertha to survive. I simply had to let go. As you've read, letting go, to me, meant a great many things. Beautiful things. But also, shameful things.

Lying on the bed, I stared out the door into the hall. I hoped I wouldn't see any of those state inmates. It wasn't unusual to wake up on any particular morning and find one of the state prisoners wandering our floor, rifling through dresser drawers. This particular halfway house assigned all its federal inmates to the fourth floor. It was on the other three floors where the District of Columbia and state inmates were housed.

I don't mean to sound snobby here, but federal inmates seemed to be more honorable in their crimes. They didn't commit crimes against a person, usually against an institution, like a credit union, bank, or in my case, the government au-pair program. We liked to think of ourselves as honorable criminals, and again, in my case, I didn't see myself as a criminal at all. One of the inmates on the second floor was awaiting her sentence for beating her infant baby to death. Wow, that's not something you would ever come across in federal prison, unless, that is, a person did it at the post office, which is federal property. I just didn't like the feeling I had every time I had to walk down the stairs to the second floor. I had lived with criminals, mostly drug-related, for over a year now and never felt the compulsion to confront someone over their crime as I did now. It made me sick to my stomach at the thought of her beating that baby. I dared not say anything to her; in addition to getting me in trouble with the halfway house, she'd probably beat me to death. She was a bully, period. And I certainly didn't want to hear that she was on drugs and that made her do it.

I stayed away from the second floor as much as I could. I had enough to do with the constant regulation of everything we did. Every woman was given bathroom duty each week; the cleaning supplies were generic ammonia and Windex. There was a bathroom on every floor, and there were four floors. I would awake each morning to the smell of ammonia. Every morning, some woman was scrubbing away in the bathroom, leaving behind that lingering smell.

This following morning was my favorite, "Pancake Day," so I dashed around to get ready and made a beeline to the kitchen. Our halfway house had an elderly black woman who came in daily to cook for us misfits. She arrived around six am and made breakfast, lunch, and dinner. We all loved her. She was a large woman with folds under her chin, and she always wore her hair in a bun. Boy, she could cook!

After breakfast, I had to map out a plan for my counselor on how I was going to go about finding a job. A job! I hadn't thought about a job even once while I was in prison. In prison, all you think about is getting through the loneliness of the day. You concentrate on the now, not the future. But today I had to sit down with my counselor and think about my future. I had no idea where to begin. I was experienced in raising children, running an illegal au-pair service, and working in a gym (I had worked in the prison gym). I really was more underqualified than some sixteen-year-olds.

My counselor came in and asked me what I would do to find a job. That was a good question, but I didn't have a good answer. In prison, everything was decided for me, but now someone was asking me to think for myself. And what did I want to do for employment? I wasn't exactly feeling very ambitious. The ambition had been sucked right out of me. Honestly, I just wanted to find a sunny island, sit on the beach, and drink wine coolers all day. Find a Tiki bar and make new friends. Employment? No, I didn't want a job! Why does everyone think people released from prison are so eager to get back into the workforce? Prison is terribly hard work. What I wanted was a vacation. Considering the newspapers at my front door, BBC's "Spotlight" interview giving me the opportunity to make a fool of myself, the attorney's fees and meetings, the sheer emotions of dealing with losing family, friends, and freedom, and with the trial and sentencing, followed by acclimation to prison and adjusting to keeping myself safe inside… and now, once released, they expect you to want to go to work? I was exhausted physically and emotionally… that lovely, sunny island.

I began to wonder about the qualifications of my counselor. In prison most of the guards had bachelor's degrees; the Bureau of Prisons sought out degreed employees. But my counselor that day had poor grammar and looked like a pimp. Think every cliché actor you saw on TV in the 70s dressed like a pimp, and that would be the man sitting in front of me. Maybe I could do his job?

I sat in that room with this counselor, a dark room that smelled like an old woodpile. I had no idea what to tell him. My sinuses were starting to bother me since the room had no ventilation and no windows. It was one of the smaller rooms; I suppose it would have been considered a waiting room when it was built in the early 1900s. I don't think it was intended to have furniture.

Suddenly, sitting in front of this halfway house counselor, I started to sneeze. After each "God bless you," I sneezed again. It turned into a sneezing frenzy. One right after the other. Finally, the "God-bless-you" to all my sneezes stopped, replaced with, "What's wrong with you?" I told him the room had no ventilation, was full of dust and smelled. He just looked at me, rolled his eyes and waited for my sneezing to stop. With my eyes still watering, he told me he would give me to the end of the month, June, to find employment. After that, he would find it for me. I could only imagine what he would find. I had to find something on my own and fast. But what the hell could I do? I had been self-employed for the last fifteen years and had not worked in an office for over twenty years.

Someone suggested I work for McDonald's, but I didn't want to insult McDonald's employees with my presence. I'm a slow learner on jobs like that, and I would have pissed off the person training me because I couldn't get an order straight. I've noticed that most fast food workers are young and energetic. I was getting slower and slower even though I was only forty-three. The poor teenager training me would have been exasperated.

As the weeks went on, I finally broke down and called a friend who was an accountant and pleaded with him and his wife to hire me as their flunky. They obliged and were quite nice about it. They did it as a favor. They actually had to think up work for me to do. Didn't get paid much, but at least I got the counselor off my back and had a job. And money wasn't a real issue at the time, since Mike my soon to be ex-husband, was paying me alimony.

CHAPTER 5

"HEY, WELCOME BACK, JANIE," Dr. Marks began. "Wasn't sure you were coming back at all. Thought I was going to have to call on the big guys, you know the federal marshals, and that would have turned into an all-out manhunt for you—I mean woman-hunt—nationwide, of course, and then they would have had to put your picture up in the post office. Well, it would have been ugly!"

"You make fun," I replied, "but believe me, one little mistake with the government or worse, and they think you've made a mockery out of them. Hell, that sort of thing *could* happen. Wouldn't have thought so years ago, but now… I believe it now."

Dr. Marks picked up a file from his desk. "I've got a lot of reading to catch up on in the event you don't want to talk again. Even brought you some magazines so you wouldn't be bored. You like *People* magazine or *Psychology Today*?"

"Same as last time. Hey, Doc, how many psychiatrists does it take to change a light bulb?" He just shrugged. I answered for him, "Just one, but the light bulb has to want to change."

Dr. Marks smiled. "Good one, Janie. Did you make that up?"

"No, just read it. Reminded me of you and all the other shrinks I've seen in my lifetime."

"How could I remind you of anyone, Janie, since you haven't even had a conversation with me?"

"Oh, I can tell," I answered. "I can just tell. You're all the same."

"And are all inmates the same, Janie?"

"In some ways. We all broke the law. But some of us own it and admit it and others just sit and blame and deny."

"Oh, so you're not all the same, are you? Don't you know by now that there are never two things exactly alike? I thought since you knew everything, you would know that as well. But maybe you don't have all the answers, and neither do I. Is it me, or do you just want to have some control over what is going on here?"

"It's you."

"Thought so. Well, can't win them all."

Dr. Marks sat down and started going through a file. He eventually put his glasses on top of his head and looked over at me. "Let me tell you something, Janie. You may think you're controlling this situation by being silent, but you're actually letting anger control you. Can you see that?"

"No, I actually can't."

"Janie, I can't read minds, and I don't have a crystal ball, so talk to me. The only reason you want to sit in silence is to show that no one can make you talk. And you want to control this because you're angry. Don't get me wrong. If I were in your position, I'd probably be pretty pissed off as well. But you're letting your anger control this."

He was right, of course, and I hated to admit it. I was hugely pissed off. Spending time in prison, losing everything I ever owned, my family all spread apart, my children resenting me, and now being court ordered to see a shrink. Hugely pissed off. "Yeah, I am pissed."

"I can see that. You're like a time bomb ready to explode, tick, tock, tick, tock… you get the idea?"

"And you're going to pull the fuse?"

"Well, I'm not the bomb squad, but I would like to talk to you about it. I'm truly interested in what you have to say. I don't get many soccer moms in here who've been sent to prison. Let's just say, I'm all ears."

I did want to talk. I just didn't know where to begin. I felt that if I started to open up, I would spill out my entire being and would have to be mopped up at the end of the day. I was pissed, and that was all I could feel. I was thinking that if I sat in silence it would piss him off as well, and then we could be pissed off together. But it wasn't working; he was reading instead of being pissed off. Now, that just pissed me off all the more.

I looked over at him and winked a small wink, as I had that day in the courtroom when the reporter asked me after sentencing what I was going to do about childcare while in prison. Dr. Marks caught the wink and smiled. "Okay, Ms. Janie, let's start by breaking down what you told me last week. Let's begin with, 'I got sick.' Tell me how you got sick, and please make it interesting; I've got a long day ahead of me, and I'm not in the mood for boring stories."

"Fuck you! I don't care if you're entertained or not. In fact, I just changed my mind; I'm not telling you anything."

"You got the 'fuck you' down pat, that's for sure. Do you think I'm the enemy, Janie? That I single-handedly put you in prison? That I conspired with the government to have you arrested and put away?"

"I don't know. Did you?" I was smiling.

"You know, maybe I can help. I'm known as a good listener and have at times given good advice. Talk to me for a little while, and if you begin to get bored with me or you really don't like me, then walk away. At least then you can say you gave it a try."

"Where's the couch?"

"Sorry, just chairs, uncomfortable chairs. It's all I can afford."

"Figures the damn government would send me to a piss-poor therapist who can't even afford a couch. You must have been the bargain of the day. How much are they paying you, anyway?"

"None of your business, Janie."

"Come on, I want to know. What am I worth on the open market?"

"Believe me, Janie, you're not that important to be on the open market."

"And why the hell would the government even care to send me to a therapist? I'm not a serial killer, for damn sake. I committed a small-ass crime and was sent away for a big-ass sentence of nearly two years. Now that screwed me up. And now the government wants to unscrew me and send me off to a shrink? Now that's fucked up."

"A lot of things are fucked up, Janie. Getting sick is fucked up. Children dying is fucked up. Men and women dying in war is fucked up. People starving in this world is fucked up. You want to talk fucked up? You've come to the right person. You think you're special in being fucked up? Sorry to break this to you, Janie, you're not! I see dozens of people who are fucked up. Fucked up from their childhood, fucked up from drugs, marriages, and being abandoned. So, let's talk about being fucked up. Let's see if you get the prize. And who, Janie, ever told you life was fair?"

"Oh, no one. I figured that one out all by my lonesome. I found out early that life wasn't going to be fair. Found that out in kindergarten. In kindergarten, my teacher would call out our names alphabetically to see what play station we wanted to play in for the day. There was one coveted play station we all wanted: The Rocky Boat. It only held four people and once in the Rocky Boat, the boys and girls would rock back and forth and squeal in delight. But my last name being Miller, by the time she got to me, all the spots were taken up in the Rocky Boat. Now that seemed unfair, but that didn't teach me about the unfairness in life. Oh no, what happened next did. One day this teacher announced that she was changing things up in roll call in order to be fair to everyone. She went on to say that previously all the spots were taken up in the Rocky Boat before others ever had a chance to play in it.

"I got all excited, and I just knew this would be my opportunity to ride in this little Rocky Boat. So, the teacher opens up her book and starts doing roll call in reverse order. She started at the end of the alphabet. But, my name being Miller, I still fell in the middle and NEVER got to ride that damned Rocky Boat. Right then and there, I saw life was not fair. So, you see, I figured that out for myself and at a young age."

"Touching story, Janie, but I think children dying of disease and starving is much more unjust."

I didn't like what he had just said, and I didn't like his tone. But he was right. I didn't have the market cornered on being screwed in the head and screwed over by the government—not by a long shot. He was seeing through my bullshit. I began to like him... A LOT!

I actually found myself wanting to talk to him. "Let me say that most of my mental problems began with panic attacks after smoking pot. I don't know if the pot caused the panic attacks or not, but that's when they began. And what's worse, the panic attacks continued even when I wasn't smoking. Go figure that one out."

"Janie, a lot of people who are anxious, and I'm assuming you are, have high levels of anxiety in their brain activity. I've read where marijuana can flip the switch to acute panic attacks and sometimes delusions. Obviously, this doesn't happen to everyone, because if it did, no one would smoke pot, but in many cases, many cases that people don't like to talk about, marijuana *is* the catalyst for intense panic attacks."

"Then why all the panic attacks when I wasn't smoking?"

"I believe it's because, at that point, your neurotransmitters got out of whack. You created a chemical imbalance in your brain with smoking marijuana and that might have caused the intense panic attacks. Hard to digest, right? Who would think a drug intended for relaxation and 'fun' could cause so much havoc in the brain?"

"You mean if I hadn't smoked the pot, the panic attacks would have never happened?"

"Oh, I'm not saying that. Maybe there would have been another catalyst that flipped the switch. We'll never know. But it's pretty safe to say that in your case, it was the marijuana that flipped the switch. Let's end today and take it up next week. But before you go, I have two questions for you."

"Just two?"

"Yeah, just two. The first one is, do you know how it feels to be pushed out of an airplane without a parachute?"

"Obviously not!"

"I think you do. And my last question, how did you feel about yourself after experiencing these panic attacks?"

"I have to think about that one. To tell you the truth, I don't want to remember."

"Try."

"Alright, I felt like a loser. I felt defeated. I felt confused. I felt anxious about the next panic attack. I felt helpless. I felt embarrassed. Does that answer your question?"

"Yes, it does, Janie. And that makes sense to me. See you next week. Oh, and by the way, thank you."

"Thank you for what?"

"For not making me have to read all those boring journals. Your stories are much more interesting."

The following weeks I spent time seeing Dr. Marks and my children. I also worked for my friend. By this time summer had set in, and everyone wanted to stay indoors in air conditioning. Central air in an old halfway house can have some strange smells. The air didn't always quite make it up to the fourth floor and most times I would have to sleep without a sheet or comforter. Between the smells of ammonia, Windex, and leaky refrigerant, I was getting nauseated. But I was glad to be out of prison, so I worked on counting my blessings.

One morning, one of the state inmates who lived on one of the lower floors woke me and asked for my urine. My urine? "Yeah," she kept saying, "go into the bathroom and pee in this jar."

I sat up and looked at her and, of course, I knew why she wanted it. In federal prison, we were spot-checked, urine on demand, to see if we were taking drugs. There was no way a person could get another's urine. But in the halfway house, urine checks were announced, which made no sense; in this case, a thirty-something woman approached me, wanting mine, holding out a jar. "Here's how it goes, Cochran," she said with a faint threat in her voice. "I'm going to pour it out of this jar and into this tube and stick this tube into my pants, thus having it reach down to my crotch. So, when I sit on the toilet, I'll pinch off the top of the tube, and it'll look like I'm peeing from my pee hole. Get it?"

Yeah, I got it. No way was I going to mess up my release date for this third-floor inmate. She was crazy. "No, not doing it," I told her.

"Okay, we'll trade," she said. "How about $10 for one pee?"

"Don't need the money," I answered.

"How about I give you some oral sex?" she shot back.

"Interesting and ridiculous," I replied. "Don't need that either," I added.

"Oh, you got someone diggin' ya?" she asked.

"Ha," I answered, "come back to me when I'm ninety, I might need you then. Look, you don't have anything I want or need. You're not getting my pee, so go away."

"Ungrateful little bitch," she muttered as she walked away.

I saw her working the floors and presumed she found someone to buy off for her urine, because as far as I knew she was never busted.

My two boys were living with their father in a small suburb in Maryland, only thirty minutes from D.C. My daughter Micah was living with my parents temporarily in a small town in Missouri. She had planned to return to Maryland in the fall and register for the eighth grade if she wanted to come back. I didn't know how the kids felt about me anymore. I had turned their lives topsy-turvy. Sending my daughter to live with my mother was a 50/50 gamble.

While I knew my mother would take good care of her physically, my mom could be very punishing of someone's shortcomings. My daughter was going into eighth grade, the last year of middle school, and was insecure. Would my mom shame her for her insecurity or nurture her? Well, I can tell you now, since it's behind me. She nurtured her *and* shamed her. Same as she had done to me as a child, nurtured her with love, good meals, and by taking good care of her. But she just as easily ripped that away with shaming. At the time my daughter was somewhat overweight, and my mother couldn't stand that. She shamed her over her weight, which turned into an eating disorder for my daughter in her adulthood. Should I have known better than to send her there? Yes. I sent her there because I thought my mom would give her individual attention. She got the attention all right, all good and all bad.

While my daughter was still in Missouri, I would travel to see my boys in Maryland. On the days I could leave the halfway house, I would take the subway. My older son, Joshua, was in high school; the younger, Bryson, was still in elementary school. In the afternoon I would see my friend about job duties, and then I would have to leave in order to get back to the halfway house by nine pm. My husband Mike—we were still trying to figure out where we stood with one another—was now living like a bachelor. His new house had a large dog pen in the middle of the family room, and he had clothes thrown around each room. Quite a contrast to our big home in the suburbs that I had meticulously decorated and kept clean. He had a rather large dog, Sandy, a mixed lab with sandy-colored hair who loved everyone. She would jump on you and lick your face every time you walked through the door. The boys loved her. But, honestly, she got on my nerves. If I opened a door, even only to check the mail, she would jump out and go wild through the neighborhood, not returning for hours. A couple of times, neighbors came to Mike's door to complain about her running loose. But Sandy was free-spirited and hard to control. Once she saw that front or back door open, she made a run for it. A couple of hours later, there she would be, sitting at the front door waiting to be let in.

As for my boys, they seemed to be adjusting well to their new environment, but their lives had changed so much. In addition to dealing with separated parents, they also had been separated from their mother and sister for the last year and a half. Their beloved grandparents, both sets, had moved across the country and now my boys had to rely one hundred percent on their dad. He was a good man and did an outstanding job of stepping up to the plate. Their rooms weren't as clean as I had kept them, their house wasn't as clean as I had kept it, but they had a home and they had their own rooms. And that wasn't thanks to me. I was happy to have a husband who was responsible and caring. I would have to figure out later if we could continue in the marriage.

However, I wasn't ready to face what my children must have been feeling. I knew they felt sad and confused over my going to prison and most likely felt abandoned by me. I had to find a way to get them into counseling. When a parent, in my case, a mother, lets her children down in such a colossal way, it feels like a part of her died, and there is no coming back from it. The remorse and guilt that lives inside of you, you just want to take a knife and cut it out. Every time you look in their eyes, you imagine them thinking, "Thanks, Mom, you giant fuck-up. Look what you did to me."

I think most parents start off believing they will be the best parents ever. I will never do to them what my mom or dad did to me. They will have a better life; I will see to that. I will play baseball with them, take them to ballet, do their homework with them, never neglect them. And then, Boom! Some, like me, fail in all areas. Then the guilt sets in like a slow-moving shadow enveloping your being. It finally takes hold and you're a hostage to the guilt.

Then in my case, I started playing Disneyland mom. "Oh, you want this?" I can get that. I began to think material things could make up for the mistakes I had made. I would move heaven and earth to get them that one little material thing they desired.

One morning, coming from the halfway house, I walked into my boys' room and I saw my older one laughing his head off and my younger one screaming. I saw where Josh, the older one, had put a large blanket over the dog pen which stood in the middle of the room. Josh was poking a large stick through the wires of the pen. My younger one, Bryson, and a friend of his were in the pen, scrambling from one end to the other so as not to be poked hard by that stick. I threw everything I was carrying on the floor, ran over to the pen and opened the gate so they could get out. When I looked closely, I could see the boys in the pen were laughing, coughing, and screaming, all at the same time.

"Aw," said Josh, "we're just having fun."

"Fun?'" I shouted. "You could have poked their eyes out."

"Nah," he responded, "they know when to get away from the stick." And with that, they were all talking about putting Josh in the pen and doing the same to him. I saw him hunch down, getting ready to go in. I grabbed his arm and screamed, "Enough!"

Had my boys gone insane since I left? Probably not. But for nearly two years, I wasn't used to being around them. I'd forgotten how you had to keep an eye on them twenty-four/seven. I hadn't parented them for such a long time. Even before prison, I hadn't been there for them emotionally during my mania/depression. So, I had many things to learn now that I was back both physically and mentally.

My daughter told me that on the night I was sent away to prison, she went through my things, putting everything away, when she ran across my cloth headband which I used to hold my hair back when I washed my face. She said she took the headband and sat down with it on the bathroom floor, held it up to her face, smelled my scent and cried. She and her older cousin brought it to me that very same night when I chose to spend my last night of freedom with my boyfriend and friends having a last hoorah drinking and laughing the night away. My then ten-year-old little girl felt me hug her goodbye, an evening too soon, to spend what time I had left with people who entertained me.

Micah later told me she was overwhelmed with sadness and grief that night. Her world would change so much over the long course of my absence, and she would feel abandoned by me. How could I have explained it all to her, what I had done, and the mania which drove me? Could a child understand mental illness? No. I didn't think she would understand until she became an adult, and I just prayed she didn't totally hate me by that time.

I returned to the halfway house one evening. I climbed into bed and started reading a magazine. I think it was *Glamour* since I recall being enthralled about some new make-up tip. Then, BAM! I was startled by the sound of footsteps coming up the winding stairs. BOOM, BOOM, BOOM, the footsteps were getting closer and closer. I looked around at my roommates, and we just looked back at one another and shrugged. And then, BOOM! Our door swung open and there stood four federal marshals, wearing their government-issued uniforms and badges.

"Everyone out of the room and in the hallway. NOW!" one of them shouted.

I put my magazine down and headed out the door. What in the world? They left the door open so we could all see what was going on in the room. They went over to one of my roommates' area and started tossing everything of hers into green plastic bags: her clock, magazines, books, make-up, jewelry, and picture frames, and then they stripped her bed, throwing her sheets and comforter into a plastic bag. Within ten minutes they were done. They had annihilated every trace of this woman's presence. They walked out and told us we could re-enter the room. We were all startled. Where was this roommate they had just erased? She was gone, just like that.

It didn't take long before the whole story unfolded. In the halfway house you are given privileges, like weekend passes. But privileges only last with appropriate behavior. It turns out this particular roommate had dirty urine, so the federal marshals were called in. They packed her up and shipped her right back to federal prison. No second chances, Boom-Bang, and you're gone. Really scared the shit out of me.

CHAPTER 6

"HI, DOC," I SAID to Dr. Marks. I had decided to be friendlier this go-round. I was beginning to really like this doctor. I liked the way he cut to the chase.

"Hey, been waiting for you. Sit down. Let me ask you something. When you finally did see a psychiatrist, who did you see?"

"Oh, some guy over in Annapolis. Remember, this was 1974, and the term 'panic attack' wasn't even coined yet. As I said, society and psychiatry thought people who claimed to have had panic attacks were just being hysterical."

"Well, what did *you* think?"

"I thought I was insane."

"And now?"

"And now what?" I asked.

"What do you think about all this now?"

"I think I'm screwed up and don't know whom to blame."

"Well," he said, "that's important to get to the bottom of. We have to find someone to blame, and it can't be us, right?" We both started to laugh. "What did you tell the psychiatrist back in '74?" he continued.

"I told him I was having these terrifying thoughts or moments and didn't know why. I told him it felt as if I were on some LSD trip gone bad, that I first experienced this feeling while smoking pot. He looked across the desk, adjusted his glasses up his nose and said, 'Well, young lady, I advise you not to smoke any more marijuana.' Gee, I thought, at least I wanted to hear it was all my parents' fault." We both laughed.

"Do you feel it was your parents' fault?" Dr. Marks asked.

I looked around the room and then at him, and replied, "Do I think being screwed up is my parents' fault? Yeah, why not?" I replied. "Everything is my mom's fault, not my dad's; he's perfect."

Dr. Marks smiled and said, "No one is perfect, Janie."

"Oh," I said, "Jesus was."

"Aw!" he replied. "Now we're bringing religion into this. Well, I wouldn't know anyway; I'm Jewish."

"I don't know who to blame, what to think. All I know is that...."

"Let me finish this," he insisted. "You got sick, saw some doctors, and they told you to take these pills. You took them and got crazier, and then committed a crime, went to prison, and were court ordered to see me. "Also," he went on, "Steve Miller was singing, 'Keep on Rocking Me' on the radio the entire time."

I put my hands under my arms and responded, "Well, I see you can read minds now. Please continue."

"No," he said, "I'd rather you take it from where you got sick. Fill me in on all the missing details."

"What details?" I responded.

"Details like when and where you were born."

"Why do you care?" I retorted.

"Well, let me think about that one, Janie. I'm a psychologist. I 'm paid to analyze you, and to do that I have to know where you began. So, why in the world wouldn't I care?"

"So, what do you want to know?"

"I just told you. When and where were you born?"

"I was born in Illinois in 1954, but I'm sure you know that. Raised for my first fifteen years in Illinois and Missouri. Moved to Maryland with my parents when I was fifteen years old. But I have a sneaky feeling you know that as well."

"How would I know that?"

"From the friggin' court papers, that's how."

"Maybe I read them, and maybe I didn't," he replied. "They can be so boring, you know what I mean?"

"Oh, great, the government sent me to an incompetent psychologist!"

"Don't be a smart ass. Just answer my questions, please. How many siblings do you have?"

"I have one brother, Terry, and he's two years older."

"Do you see your mom, dad, and brother often?"

"I see my mom and dad a couple of times a year; they live in Missouri, I live in Maryland. I see my brother more often because he lives here. What else do you want to know?"

"Alright. We'll end for the day. But I want you to start thinking about why you blame yourself so intensely for your pain."

"And who else is there to blame but me? I was always taught that what I feel or am experiencing is all up to me. So, if I'm feeling unstable, then naturally it had to be my fault. I remember at a young age my family making comments that so-and-so was crazy and that he had the power to snap out of it. It was always the person's fault who was the alcoholic, drug addict, or mentally ill. It was never just the circumstances or just the cards they were handed. Oh, no! That person had something to do with it. Mental illness was seen in my family as one big guilt trip. If you were mentally ill, then you did something to cause it. So, why wouldn't I blame myself for my condition? No one else to blame it on. Not even God."

"Blame's an important part of your thinking process, isn't it, Janie? I mean, you really want to be able to blame someone or something for all of this. Why is that?"

"Because, good doctor, I want to be guilt free. If it's my fault, if I'm to blame, then I feel guilty. People are always told that they can change the way they feel. But I can't do it! My brain is screwed up, and I can't change it. Society tells me it's my fault because I have the power to change my thoughts. So, if I can't, it has to be my fault."

"Your family tells you that as well, don't they, Janie? Your family tells you that if you're not behaving a certain way or if you're thinking a certain way that isn't a part of their norm, then there has to be something wrong with you? Am I right?"

"Yes," I hollered, "you're right! I hid this condition for years upon years from my parents, friends, coworkers, boyfriends, EVERYONE! And why? Because I felt defective and guilty about it! That's why!"

"If you had had a heart problem, would you blame yourself? If you had bad knees, would you blame yourself? No, you probably wouldn't. But it's interesting that when it comes to the brain, everyone, like you, clams up and starts blaming himself. Guess what, Miss Janie? It isn't your fault. Do you hear me? It isn't your fault. Has anyone ever told you that before?"

I nodded yes. "I had been told that before by another psychiatrist that I had seen years earlier. That was the psychiatrist that over-medicated me, which led me down the rabbit hole. But he had told me repeatedly it wasn't my fault." I looked up at Dr. Marks and added, "Yes, I've been told that."

"But you don't believe it, do you?"

I shook my head no.

"Pity. So much of your life has been eaten up with thoughts of guilt. So many opportunities might have been passed up over guilt. Guilt can eat a person up alive. There are probably things in your life that you can blame yourself for; mental illness is not one of them."

CHAPTER 7

I HEARD THE EAR-SHATTERING noise of thunder as I ran down the street to Mike's house. I was afraid lightning was going to strike me, so I ran that much faster. When I got there, I was soaking wet. It was one of those hot summer rains that hit around the end of July. I had left the halfway house two hours prior.

I was running late that day and didn't get to Mike's until mid-afternoon. My boys had their bags packed and were anxiously waiting to go. Sandy was running around in circles wanting to go out-side and play in the rain. I was in no mood to chase her down the street if she got out, so I barked out orders to the boys to watch her and make sure she didn't escape.

Today was the day the boys headed to my parents' home in Missouri, where my daughter was staying, to spend a month with their grandpar-ents. I was to take them to the airport, but I forgot something, something I forgot on purpose, something I wasn't allowed to forget. I knew I would have to pay, but I put it out of my mind as I loaded their suitcases in the trunk, and off we went. It was pouring rain when I hit Baltimore, and I could barely see out the windshield. Bryson was in the back seat nearly crying, fearful I would have to pull over and they would miss their flight. The rain subsided for a moment, and I finally arrived at Baltimore-Wash-ington International. We parked and headed for the terminal.

I watched as my boys walked down the jetway to the airplane, and I said a silent prayer that they would arrive in one piece in Missouri. I was nervous about them flying. I know driving is more dangerous statistically than flying, but for the life of me I couldn't figure out how they kept that fifty-ton piece of metal in the air. One time a screw fell out of a wing, or something like that, and the whole fucking plane went down in flames. I just didn't want the fate of my sons resting on one fucking screw. Oh, well. I watched as the plane taxied away from the gate. I knew I had to shake it off.

When I arrived back at Mike's house, his phone was ringing. It was the main counselor, a female case manager from the halfway house. She said she'd been trying to reach me all afternoon and demanded to know where I had been. I was caught… again. Halfway house rules forbid you to do any extracurricular activities outside your job unless you have prior permission. I didn't have permission to take the boys to the airport. I told her where I had been, and she instructed me to immediately return.

I picked up my purse and headed for the bus to the subway. It had stopped raining, but it was still a gloomy dark outside. As I walked to the bus stop, I felt just as gloomy inside. I knew the punishment for breaking halfway house rules meant more confinement. I kept asking myself why I hadn't just gotten permission. I guess because I was feeling a little more freedom than I should have.

Fact is that I didn't want to ask for permission. I didn't want to be reminded that my life was still being controlled. I wanted to delude myself into thinking that I was actually free. Now, standing outside waiting for the bus, I was well aware I was not in control and did not have my complete freedom returned, yet.

While waiting, a familiar face drove by in a car and stopped. It was my brother Terry. He pulled over and opened up the passenger side door. He told me to jump in, and he would drive me to the subway. He said he had gone to Mike's looking for me, saw I wasn't there and was driving home when he saw me. I asked him why he wasn't at work, and he told me he had taken a few days off for vacation. I told him what I had done, and he just smiled, patted me on my hand and said, "This, too, shall pass." Then he dropped his head, gave out a slight laugh and said, "Bonnie, when are you going to give up this life of crime?"

He dropped me off at the subway and just smiled, the same smile he had the day he came to Baltimore and bailed me out. I told him that he was always my rock and it was a Godsend that he showed up today. His presence gave me the courage to face what was awaiting me at the halfway house. My wings were about to get clipped once again.

My punishment was what I had predicted, more confinement. My weekend pass for that week was revoked. It wasn't as bad as I thought it could have been. When the weekend began, I ran out to the local grocer and bought up all the "Little Debbie's" and "Ho Ho's" I could find. Then I bought a *Glamour* magazine, *The Enquirer*, *Star* and, for good measure, *Time*. Stuck them in a bag and ran back to my room to be there by five pm Friday, when the punishment was to begin.

The next day, I sat in bed and read magazines, eating my junk food. Some of the other women felt sorry for me, so they would come in and keep me company. The weekend went by fast, and luckily my children were in Missouri, so I wasn't missing out on time with them. It was just me, the magazines, and the junk food that weekend.

When I got bored of reading, I put on the small, antique color TV that was probably bought in the 70s and watched old re-runs of *I Love Lucy*, *The Dick Van Dyke Show*, *Green Acres*, *The Beverly Hillbillies*, and, of course, my favorite, *Law and Order: Special Victims Unit*.

Time passed quickly and then came Monday. My freedom was somewhat back.

CHAPTER 8

I WAS BACK WITH Dr. Marks, but I was Okay with that. I really did like him, but let me add that it was in a *Good Will Hunting* kind of way.

"Come on in, Janie Renee," he said. "Sit down and tell me all about it."

"Fuck off!" I answered.

"Oh, I can see you're in a good mood," he said with a smile. "Let me ask you this, Janie. What do you now do for pleasure? You've been in the halfway house for, what is it, a couple of months? What do you do to entertain yourself?"

"I don't know, Dr. Marks. What do you do to entertain yourself? Jerk off?"

"Oh, now we're getting personal, are we? Whether I jerk off or don't is none of your business. Let's get one thing straight, Ms. Janie Renee, you've been ordered by the court to see ME. I'm not court ordered to answer YOUR questions."

"Well, bravo for you, Doc. Okay, just one more question. Do you still have sex with your wife?"

"Not going to answer that either, Janie. And how do you know I'm married?"

"Because I see your pictures, all lined up on the bookcase, of a little girl, who I assume is your daughter, a picture of you with a woman and a little girl, and then on top of that, you're wearing a wedding ring. So, I guess it was just a lucky guess," I said with a smile.

"Very good, grasshopper," he said with a huge smile. "Now, go back and take me forward from when you saw a psychiatrist for the first time."

"The truth is, he didn't know what the hell was going on, and so he stuck my ass in group therapy. That's what they did in the 70s. If they didn't know what was wrong with you, or if you didn't have a garden variety type of mental illness, they stuck you in group therapy. Of course, that didn't help the panic attacks, but it was interesting. Then later I got involved in a bad relationship with a drug user. He was a dealer too, every father's dream for his daughter, left my cushy job with the union and sat and zoned out with panic attacks. I started to just deal with them. I didn't know what the hell was going on with my brain, but I just had to deal with them."

"How?"

"I just told you."

"Did you do drugs with your druggy boyfriend?"

"Well, I was afraid to do pot, of course. I stayed away from pot like it was my kryptonite, but some drugs, yes."

"What kind of drugs are we talking about?"

"Like some coke. But I do have an interesting story for you, Doc."

"Oh, please do tell. I'm bored as shit at this point; if I've heard one zoned-out druggie boyfriend story, I've heard them all. Please continue, I'd like to hear a fresh one."

"On July 4th, 1975, I was on my boyfriend's ass about using drugs. He told me I needed to relax and not worry about it so much. He came into the room where I was watching TV and brought me a bowl of ice cream. Later, we left to see fireworks at a nearby park. As we sat on top of the car, the fireworks began. But as they exploded in the sky, the color became very intense. As the ashes fell to the ground, I kept freaking out that they were falling on top of me and burning me. I started to scream every time I felt ashes falling on my skin. I started to use my hands to brush off the ash; I was brushing my skin so hard it felt like it was going to peel off. I was terrorized, and panic attacks started rolling in. I couldn't catch my breath and started hyperventilating. I had to go home in a hurry. Once we got home, I curled up in a ball and started crying. I was seeing colors, and my mind was going a mile a minute. I asked my boyfriend to take me to the emergency room because I was freaking out. Freaking out again! But this time I was freaking out in Technicolor. It was so weird and frightening.

"An old black-and-white movie was on TV: Cary Grant and some woman. I started to hallucinate I was in the movie with them. To this day, I can still see myself standing by Cary Grant at an elevator. I actually injected myself into the movie on TV. I was in that TV and in that movie."

"Why wouldn't your boyfriend take you to the hospital, Janie?"

"I didn't know at the time why. He just wanted me to calm down and to stop being agitated. He would put his hands on my shoulders, and I would quickly, defensively, push them off. I called my mom. She came over and drove me to the hospital. They gave me Valium and sent me home. That was another thing they did in the 70s, everyone threw Valium at you whenever you became anxious. No tests, nothing. Just Valium. I had no friggin' idea why I freaked out so badly that night."

"Janie, where's the punch line?"

"It's coming. Twenty years later, I ran into him again."

"Janie, you didn't run into him; you had an affair with him."

"Damn those files," I said. "Damn, is there one thing about me not in there? I thought you didn't read them."

"Maybe I'm not as incompetent as you think."

I managed a weak smile. "It turns out that bastard laced my ice cream with two tabs of LSD. He watched me trip and didn't even tell me what was happening."

"What a little shit. Wrong on so many levels. He should have gone to jail."

"Can you believe that son of a bitch thought it would be interesting to see me trip my mind out while we watched fireworks. I know now why he didn't want to take me to the emergency room; he would have been arrested for drugging me. The worst of it was that for twenty years I thought it was me, that at any moment I could go off the deep end and start hallucinating."

"Janie, if your brain wasn't already miss-wired, it certainly would have been after that. Let me ask you something. Did your panic attacks after that become even more intense?"

"Why, yes, they did, Doc. Mighty intense, as they say in Texas."

"You know, LSD is known to stay in the brain for years, sometimes for the rest of your life. I'm sorry that happened to you. Very sorry. Do you know where he is today?"

"Yeah."

"Let's find him and string him up!"

"Yeah, that's a good idea."

"Janie...."

"Yeah?"

"That experience altered your life."

I had tears in my eyes. Finally, I was able to tell someone how awful that was.

"Janie, I've known patients who've had their lives altered by bad LSD trips—and they knew they took it."

"And get this, Doc, here's the cherry on top. I worked on Jimmy Carter's inaugural committee, and I pinched some tickets to the inaugural ball. Guess who I took as my date?"

"That little turd?"

"Yeah, the little, little LSD turd. If I had known then what he had done to me, I would have had him arrested."

"I don't blame you, Janie. You didn't know. But now that you do, I hope that brings some comfort to you. Three questions before we end."

"Oh, brother, what are they? No, I don't know what it's like to jump out of an airplane with or without a parachute."

"No, not that," he said, laughing.

"I just wanted to know if you enjoyed Jimmy Carter's inaugural ball."

"I did. Lots of celebrities, getting to see the President up close, and the Vice-President. The First Lady was beautiful in her gown. I really had a good time."

"Next question. How did you manage your panic attacks after the night your lovely boyfriend laced your ice cream?"

"Eventually, I just started pushing the envelope. I knew I had to start living my life and whatever happened, happened."

"And my last question is, had you ever tried LSD before that night?"

"Once," I said, "but it was when I was a teenager. It felt like I was in slow motion. Nothing like what I felt that Fourth of July."

"Every LSD experience is different, depending on the potency of the drug and how your brain interprets it. Well, I think that should wrap it up today."

I started to gear up for the fall. My children would be returning home in two weeks. I had to register my daughter in a new school and get her and my two sons ready for the new year, buying supplies and all those things good mothers do.

One day, I wandered into my halfway house counselor's office and sat down. He looked up at me and asked what I wanted. He rarely saw me in his office because I tried to keep a low profile since my arrival. That was something I learned in prison, keep a low profile at all times. Don't ask for anything, keep your head down, and try to disappear into the woodwork. I asked the counselor when would be my exact release date from the halfway house. He informed me it would be near Christmas, and then I would be on probation for another year. Yikes, I thought, when would this nightmare end?

Early September was my brother's birthday. I was on a weekend pass, so I went to the birthday party his wife threw for him. He looked so comfortable sitting in one of his recliners; he loved his recliners and his remote controls. He was two years older than I and had always managed to stay out of trouble. True, when we were kids, he hated me. I think he would have sold me to a passing carnival of gypsies if he could have gotten away with it, but now as adults, we really enjoyed each other's company. Terry was a born-again Christian, but not the Bible-thumping type. He didn't throw down the gauntlet if you didn't agree with him. He simply lived the life of a Christian instead of just preaching about it. One could learn from his example. And what I mean is that his life seemed so peaceful. Not that he didn't have every-day stress, but he had a certain calmness about him and an easygoing attitude. He attributed that to Jesus and God. I would look at him, as I did this day, and just thank God he was in my life.

As children, we were raised in the strictness of the Baptist church, fire, and brimstone all around us. Our parents were easygoing, but in church, some of the parishioners were very judgmental and harsh. But Terry found his way and still managed to find peace in his beliefs. I was hoping some of that would rub off on me.

I looked around his small townhouse and wondered why he hadn't bought a bigger place for himself, his wife and daughter. He had two sons from a previous marriage, and they lived on their own. He had a large-screen TV with five remotes; he just loved those remotes. He had two state-of-the-art recliners and a nice sofa. He lived on his electrician's income and his wife's nursing salary. They definitely didn't live above their means. He was happy, and it showed that day during his birthday party. All he really wanted out of life at this point was more remotes—

Okay, I'm kidding—but what he really wanted was for the ones he loved in life to be just as peaceful and content as he was. I wanted that for myself and my children as well.

My three children were at the party, and they had fun hanging out with their cousin Allison. As I watched them play, I couldn't help but think of how much sadness and havoc I had managed to bring into their lives. They had hitched their star to my wagon, and my wagon went astray. Now, I was in the process of getting it back on track. I was so sorry for what I had done to them. The oldest ones were in high school now and the youngest in elementary school. They deserved and needed stability. I needed to be up to the job.

I was surprised when Terry came over to me where I was sitting, in a recliner of course. He kicked back his feet in the other recliner and abruptly asked me about my love life. I was separated from Mike, on the verge of divorce, and Terry wanted to know if I were dating anyone. I didn't think he would approve if I replied in the affirmative, so I just told him, "No."

He looked over at me, pushed his glasses down his nose so his eyes were peering over the top, and said, "Janie, this is me you're talking to, now give me the dirt."

So, I let my guard down and told him about Chris, someone I thoroughly enjoyed being with, but who had control problems of his own. Chris wanted to control all my movements. And I wasn't even sure I was in love with him.

Terry said he wanted Mike and me to give it another chance, but as usual, didn't judge me. He just patted me on the hand as he usually did and said, "Be careful." And with that, he was up out of his recliner, meeting and greeting his well-wishers.

The following week I got the children enrolled in school and looked into getting them into long-term counseling. Mike had excellent insurance, and it didn't take me long before I found the counselors I was looking for. In the meantime, Chris and I were still seeing one another. I enjoyed Chris, up to a point. But it came to a screeching halt one day when I came home from the grocery store.

Chris had said he was going to meet me at Mike's and pick me up to go to a movie. But when I got back from the store, Chris was sitting in his car in Mike's driveway. I got out of my car and asked him to help me bring in the groceries. He obliged but was quiet the entire time. Once we got into the house, he demanded to see my grocery receipt. I kind of laughed and dug for it in my purse. I held it up in the air, just out of his reach, waved it around and laughingly asked why he wanted to see it. He moved in closer and snatched it out of my hands. He looked it over, and while he was examining it, he said he was checking for the time when they rang up the order. He wanted to see if I had gone somewhere else after having gotten the groceries. Talk about my eyebrow going up; both eyebrows went up for that one.

Now, I'm the kind of person who never heeds red flags, and it has to get ridiculously bad for me to exit a relationship, but I was just too tired for this kind of action. Chris and I did see each other after that day but on a dwindling basis. Eventually, he and I parted as friends. And to this day we are still good friends.

CHAPTER 9

"JANIE, SO, LET'S SUMMARIZE," Dr. Marks began. "You saw a psychiatrist, he put you in group therapy, you went on an LSD trip, and you dated a drug dealer. Where did it go from there?"

"I ditched the dealer and met a wonderful man six years younger, and while now that would be no big deal, in 1978 it was. No one in my age group was dating younger men. I was looked at like a freak. I was twenty-four, and he was only eighteen."

"Oh, robbing the cradle?"

"Shut the fuck up! I liked him. Besides being very good-looking, he was so different from the druggie, different from all the other boys I knew in high school. He seemed very mature for his age. He was a Christian man, had high morals, did no drugs, and he accepted my craziness. I didn't understand what my problem was, but he seemed to want to put up with it. He was in love with me, and I was in love with him. I saw a future with him. And a person, like me, who suffers mentally with a disorder of any kind, feels like damaged goods. I didn't feel I had the option to be picky. I felt lucky that this man even accepted me at all. Don't even bother telling me that my self-image was poor. I'll beat ya to the punch on that one.

"Tell me, Dr. Marks, how can one's self-image be positive if he or she is mentally ill and suffering from panic attacks and depression?

How's that even possible? When you suffer from mental disorders and deep depression, you're the unlucky one, the one that no one wants to listen to. No one except your psychiatrist."

"I agree, Janie. And you know that's because most people are afraid of mental illness and depression. I think it's because they don't understand it whatsoever. Society as a whole doesn't accept what it doesn't understand."

"Not to mention, Dr. Marks, how critical and judgmental our society has become. My own family sat in judgment over my illness. My mom would ask me not to mention my mental problems with other family members. It was viewed by my family as embarrassing. Not by my brother or my dad, but by my mother and her sisters. And my illness and the consequences were fodder for much gossip among my family and friends."

"So, you got married."

"Yes. I was twenty-five at the time, and he was nineteen. It mortified my mother. She was so prim and proper, and this was so much out of the norm. Most of my friends looked at me as if I were crazy."

"Which you were, of course. Right?"

"Yeah, right," I said with a chuckle. "The wedding was beautiful. My mother pulled out all the stops. Bridesmaids, flowers, music, everything."

"But, of course, your mother controlled everything, right?"

"Yeah, she did. But it was beautiful."

"I guess you felt safe with a man who was understanding of your problem. What kind of work did he do?"

"He was going to school for computers, and back then it was a hot field."

"Then what?"

"After we got married, I landed a job as a placement director with a technical school. Once my husband graduated, I placed him in an excellent job."

"Good going."

"I wasn't experiencing so many panic attacks at the time, but I knew they were just below the surface. I still feared them. They were always looming over me. I was twenty-eight and wanted a family, so we got pregnant."

"Were you seeing a psychiatrist at the time?"

"No. What would have been the use? He would have only stuck me in group therapy, and that wasn't the answer. Group therapy may have made me feel that I wasn't alone, or gotten me some understanding, but it would not have done anything to solve my brain-chemistry problem. I still didn't know what was happening in my brain. I would have panic attacks from time to time but had a safe place to land in my husband. It was very comforting."

"You're not married to him now, are you?"

"No. You know that, so why ask?"

"Why did you get a divorce, Janie?"

"I screwed up. He screwed up. And the screwups were unfixable. Leave it at that."

"I will, for the time being, Janie, but we have to talk about it. So, you got pregnant. Happy?"

"Thrilled. Had a son, then turned around and had a daughter. My husband was working full time in the computer field and was excelling."

"And what were you doing?"

"Raising two small children. And five years after my daughter was born, I had my third child, another boy. I was very happy."

"That's when you started your business?"

"Yeah, I did. As you already damned well know, a business that made me very happy, but in the end landed me in prison."

CHAPTER 10

"HEY, JANIE, HAVE A seat and let's get rolling. I got a plane to catch. Last week you were about to tell me about the business you started."

"Seriously? You've got a plane to catch?"

"No, I'm just bullshitting you. But let's start talking."

"I don't want to."

"And why is that?"

"Because that's where all the problems began."

"How so?"

"I had a perfect life. A loving husband, a nice home, two beautiful children…."

"So, tell me about the business. What kind of business?"

"Why the hell are you doing this to me, Doc? You know exactly what kind of business. Do you think I'm so stupid as to believe it's not in the file? You sit there and ask these inane questions as if I were stupid. You pretend you don't know, but you know everything. In fact, why don't you fill me in on the details?"

"Janie, I don't know the whole story."

I sat there and just stared at him. Of course, he knew it all. The government had gone to great lengths to fill him in on everything. My whole life was an open book. I had no privacy, and everyone who was interested knew everything.

"Just tell me, Janie, what kind of business?"

"So, you can compare notes with what the government told you?"

"Yeah, is that what you want to hear? Yeah, Janie, I want to compare notes. The government doesn't always have it right. If you want to end the session for today we will, but I'm not going to sit here and drag everything out of you."

"Alright, fine. It was a babysitting referral business for damn sake. Are you happy, now? My husband and I had just moved into our new large home, and we were one big happy family until I got sick—again. I had a major breakdown. It was one big friggin' panic attack that left me sick. I was paranoid, terrorized, and helpless."

"How?"

"Terrorized. In my mind. Hard to imagine for someone who hasn't felt it. Your thoughts terrorize you. You're frozen with all blackness surrounding you. The word depression doesn't adequately describe it, Dr. Marks. When I think of the word depression, I think of being upset over a particular situation. But that's not the depths of the hell I experienced. No matter how successful I was or how much I had to look forward to, I felt like dying. Yes, dying. I felt void of any positive feelings. It's blackness. You feel separated from God. You feel hopeless that anything can fix it."

The feelings I was having at that point bring to mind how desperate my situation was. You hope that those good things you buy or experience in life will change these feelings. But when that doesn't happen, and you realize that nothing is going to take this deep darkness away, then you fixate on dying, because it's then that dying becomes a luxury. To no longer be in pain; to no longer hurt mentally; to no longer feel like you're the biggest loser that ever lived. It doesn't matter at that point how many people tell you how great you are and how much you have to live for. In fact, that only makes it worse. If everyone around you sees these wonderful things, and you don't, then you feel like there is definitely no hope for yourself. You try to cheer yourself up. I might buy something I thought I wanted, but that feeling passes soon enough. Nothing gets you excited. You end up with the darkness. And at that point, you start to ask yourself, which is worse, panic attacks or bouts of depression? At least with panic attacks, I felt alive. With the depression, I was dead inside.

And when you have exhausted consideration of all the things that people think should make you happy, and you're still not feeling happy, then you start to believe that the joy in life will be in dying. Sometimes I would think about heaven since, after all, I am a Christian. I had visions of being healthy with God, and out of pain. Being out of pain became the focal point for me when I was in the deep hole. Looking forward to heaven comforted me during these times. I would get tired of faking it in front of people, the fake laughs, the feeling like I had to entertain people, just to keep the front going. Then, of course, some relief came with alcohol. That would give me a temporary stay away from the blackness. But when the effects of the alcohol wore off, back came the darkness. It was unbearable at times. I would lie on my couch and pray for sleep, and cry out loud in my mind saying, "God, come on, throw me a lifeline… save me."

I had faith He would, and He did. I never lost faith that God would restore me, but I was in such pain waiting for that day. Every minute you're in this pain seems like an eternity. You can even hear the minute hand turn on a clock. You keep crying out, "Where's my lifeline, God? Send it before I die at my own hands." Words escape me to try to explain the pain of depression. It's mental anguish. How does one explain mental anguish? I wish at times someone had the power to open up my mind and see it. And once they saw it, they would know how to go about finding a cure. On occasion, when I came out of the dark tunnel in my mind and began to feel somewhat functional, it never felt functional enough since I was still depressed.

I became almost afraid to get out of bed in the morning. Not wanting to start my day, just lie in bed until nightfall. Turned on the TV for noise, and either ate too much or not all. I was tired and stayed tired when I was even just slightly depressed. I was sleepy and tired. And those were the good days.

But how do I feel when I am depressed? In my depression, I experience extreme self-loathing. I feel unloved. My dreams are vivid and bizarre, making sleep ineffective as an escape from my thoughts. My mind is not at rest, and I find no relief either in sleeping or staying awake. I can't read, can't focus while watching TV, and can barely hold a conversation.

I relive in my mind all bad memories from as far back as I can remember, and worst of all, I dwell on them. I feel foggy in the head and sometimes it's as if I'm viewing myself out of my body. It's a form of dissociation. There's a darkness inside of me that has enveloped my soul, and hopelessness follows. Many times, with my depression, I only see one way out of my torture chamber of thoughts and that is through death. I flirt with death and view it as a friend, not an enemy. My intrusive thoughts are maddening, and I want immediate help. It's as if a record is re-playing in my mind over and over, and I can't find the 'off' button. I completely understand why people who suffer from depression sometimes end it all with suicide. It's their escape hatch. I get it. But I wanted to live, especially for my children, so I grabbed any ounce of reassurance I could find.

As my depression deepened, I felt broken into more and more pieces. It was time to see a psychiatrist. It was 1985, and I hoped medications had improved from the 70s. Thankfully, they had. The psychiatrist I saw put me on meds, the first I'd ever taken. The doctor reassured me that if I were compliant and took the meds faithfully, I would heal and get better. I assured him I would. I went home and took the antidepressants he prescribed. I swallowed my medicine just as he said. But nothing. I felt nothing. I felt no hope. Logically, I believed I would get better because I had in the past. But the darkness in my soul told me something different.

But, as each day followed the next, I began to feel better. The self-loathing stopped, and I found interest in TV shows, movies, and books. I began conversations with people and started to move about my home. The darkness finally subsided, and I felt almost giddy; giddy in the fact that I had been falling down a bottomless well, and then I was out of the well, looking around at my surroundings. Each time I kissed my children, I did so with more dedication than the last.

I know what it feels like to be emotionally dead. Depression is an emotional death with torture. But with the help of my psychiatrist and modern medicine, the depression lifted, and I felt restored to my old self. And one thing I do less of after coming out of a depressive episode or a panic attack is not to become so judgmental and self-righteous with others. I tend to look at others with a different point of view. Others might say that they are not self-righteous, but I would beg to differ. I think we all, in some ways, are self-righteous with others every day. We look at others who have problems we can't relate to, and tell ourselves, "Well, at least I'm not that bad off." We feel better about ourselves in comparison with others. We tend to look at addicts and think, I'm not there; I didn't let myself go that low. But isn't that just another way of thinking to ourselves that we are better than those people? Which goes more to the point I'm trying to make, namely, that most of us look at others and measure our lives and self-worth compared with those of others; and the ones who fall below our standards of success get our self-righteous judgment.

Mental illness knocked all of that type of judgment and comparison out of me. I could not compare myself to anyone and feel better. My self-worth was zero once mental illness took over. I grew up in a family where outward appearances meant everything. Being considered normal was extremely important. I kept thinking when I fell ill, how can this be seen as normal? So, what I was left with was no one to compare myself with, and thus feel better about myself, even though I felt I was embarrassing my family by not looking normal. And all that adds up to shame. Shame on me, right?

Dr. Marks could see that I had dropped my defenses. I felt vulnerable, but he accepted me enough for me to rise to a new level of honesty with him. "I remember one incident," I continued, "when I was in a deep depression and put my two-year-old daughter down for a nap in her crib. I lay down in my bed next to the crib, and as she slept, I said a prayer to God. I prayed that if I were to wake up still feeling this deep darkness, that he would take my life right then and there as I slept next to my daughter. I didn't want to leave my family, but the pain was overwhelming. Then I went to sleep. My daughter woke up and started saying, 'Mommy, wake up, Mommy, wake up.' I woke up and realized God had not taken my life as I prayed for. I then had a sense of hope. I knew at that moment that if He had kept me alive, that He would find relief for me. But, oh, how I still wanted to die! I cannot begin to explain the hopelessness I felt. I wish words could explain it.

"In the darkness, I felt whispers buzzing in my head, saying, end it all. And, oh, how comforting the thought of dying was! At times it was the only thing I looked forward to. Death was my escape. I would defy my darkness by killing myself. I would show my depression who was boss. I was in complete despair every waking minute.

"And, of course, another escape was alcohol. I didn't go the conventional drug-abuse route, due to my bad experiences with illicit drugs, but I did go the alcohol route. And who could blame me? It was the only relief I found in this darkness. But finding relief in alcohol meant another darkness, an addiction called alcoholism. I didn't want two monsters in my head. Depression was bad enough, but to have to deal with addiction on top of that. No, no, no! I didn't want that. So, I tried desperately to stay away from alcohol. Sometimes I succeeded, and sometimes I didn't. And yes, there was some comfort in the antidepressants."

Dr. Marks looked at me with an openness I was sure I had not seen in him before. "Janie, being clinically depressed is an illness. No different from an illness like diabetes or any other physical ailment. I know you were hurting and in despair, but we now know how to alleviate that pain. We've come a long way in discovering medications that work effectively in treating depression. Yes, you had trouble with your antidepressants, but now you're leveled out. You feel better today because you took those medications. Am I right?"

"Yes, of course, you're right. I tried to self-medicate with alcohol, but that only made me more depressed. It just gets so dark inside your head; all you want to do is to no longer feel that pain. And alcohol numbed that pain for me. But as I said, when the effects of alcohol wore off, I was in worse shape. I was at such a point in my illness that my husband didn't know what to do with me. He insisted we go see a psychiatrist. I fought him on it, telling him it was useless, that all they would do would be throw me into group therapy. But he insisted. So, he made an appointment and drove me. He even joined me in the first session. The doctor was nice. He was working fulltime at a mental hospital. When I told him what was wrong, he assured me it was treatable. Not curable, but treatable. He used the term 'panic attack.' It was the first time I ever heard those words. He explained that my brain's electrodes were misfiring, that they were out of whack. He told me it could have been the pot that caused it, but he really didn't know. He told me that the antidepressant imipramine would put these electrodes back in order, that it would block the panic attacks and deal with the clinical depression. I didn't believe him, at first."

"Did you take the medication?"

"Damn straight I did! I would have taken anything to escape the darkness. I didn't have much faith, but I had nothing to lose. I was a waste of a person. I wasn't eating, no appetite. I was lying on my couch, out of it. I felt awful. No hope, no feeling other than the fear of panic attacks. I was in a state of mind that's hard to explain. Basically, I was non-functional. I had nothing to lose. I took those suckers every day. He told me that it would take them up to four weeks to work, and I counted every day on the calendar. I began to feel better as each day passed and counted my blessings. First, my appetite came back, and then slowly I began to feel interested in some things. Then, I began to have feelings for things in general. By the end of the fourth week, just as the doctor had prognosticated, I was whole again. My husband was thrilled."

"Did you share this with anyone other than your husband?"

"Like who? My mom didn't even know what was going on. She didn't want to. My dad was so sweet; I didn't want to confuse him. My friends thought I was going through a 'phase.' Now honestly, who would I have told? Do you think mental illness is something people want to talk about? Let me answer that. Hell, no! People don't want to hear about it, and those who have it don't want to talk about it."

Dr. Marks sat there and nodded his head in agreement. Then he looked up at me and said, "Sadly, what you say is true. We're still in the dark ages when it comes to mental illness."

"Yeah, we are, Dr. Marks. Yeah, we are."

"Janie, when you were lying on that couch in your home, and you were confused and scared, tell me how it felt."

"Alone. Suicidal and alone. I knew if the psychiatrist couldn't help me, I would end my life. I keep going back to this, but it felt like some LSD trip gone bad. The panic, the depression... I wanted to die."

"How terrifying for you, Janie. But you know what?"

"What?"

"I've had plenty of experience with others who have gone through the very same thing."

"Oh, shit. Now you want to put me in group therapy?"

He laughed. "No, not quite. I just want you to know you're not alone. Next time, Janie, I want the juice. Just how did you get here? Just how crazy over the top did you go? I want to know why the government is paying me this money."

CHAPTER 11

"OKAY," DR. MARKS SAID, "so you took your antidepressants, and on the fourth week began to feel better. In fact, you felt great. So, what was the problem?"

"I heard of a new drug, Prozac. I asked the doctor to add it to the medication I was already taking. That's where the problem began. I began to feel better than just normal, super normal... what's the word?"

"Grandiose? You began to feel grandiose?"

"I began to feel invincible. I thought every notion I had was a million-dollar idea. I was the smartest person in the room, the most creative, the one with all the visions and ideas. Yeah, Dr. Marks, grandiose. Ideas were booming in my head. I couldn't keep up with myself. I decided that my small business was small potatoes. So, I opened up an au pair service. I knew there was a market out there for nannies from Europe. An au pair can come over and work for a small fee or stipend, as they call it, of $100 per week. Now I know that sounds like a great deal, and why didn't everyone take advantage of it who needed childcare? I'll tell you why. Au pair agencies typically charge $2,500 per au pair. This includes round-trip airfare, and the au pair legally can only stay one year. So, when the year is up, the family has to pay another fee to the agency. Most average-income families find it difficult to come up with $2,500 in up-front costs, even for the first year."

"How did you know that?"

"I researched it. I found that the au pair program was started by the government as an experiment designed to help parents with the cost of daycare. But what they didn't factor in, because our government agencies aren't in touch with middle-income families, is that the ones they designed the program for couldn't afford the au pair agency fees. So, only upper-income families took advantage of the program. Typical, isn't it? Every program designed for middle-income families ends up benefiting mostly the rich."

"I don't know, if I agree with that, Janie. Not all programs end up benefitting the rich. If that were true, we wouldn't have welfare vouchers and food stamps, but I see what you're saying about the au pair program. Sad, really, middle-income families could have benefited from that."

"At the time, Dr. Marks, there were only ten sanctioned au pair agencies. When I say sanctioned, I mean only ten au pair companies that the government would allow for the program. They had an oligopoly, an almost monopoly. No one could compete against them. But I saw I could penetrate the program. There was an agency in Utah that was sanctioned to bring in au pairs. I contacted them and asked the owner how much he would charge me to bring in au pairs under his company's name, his umbrella."

"You mean, how much you would have to pay him for an au pair visa?"

"Exactly. How much would he charge me for a J-1 visa? I would find the au pair in Europe, and find families here who wanted her; all his company had to do was sign the request for the visa. He didn't even have to think about it. He immediately said, 'A thousand dollars.' And he didn't want anyone to find out about our agreement. I flew out to Utah to meet him, and wow! Did he ever have a money-making machine going! He lived in a huge home overlooking some mountains, four cars in the driveway, and in the basement was a staff of maybe five or six working on the au-pair program. I later found he had made the same arrangement with other people throughout the U.S."

"And no one found out about it?"

"Oh, hell, yes! Other agencies did find out. They were tipped off and screamed their heads off to the government. I don't blame them. But the government kept denying that I or anyone else was doing this. Now, I didn't think I was doing anything illegal. He was, I thought. I wasn't. And I wasn't even sure what he was doing was illegal. It probably just went against his agreement with the government."

"Let me see if I've got this straight. The government is allowing a near-monopoly to be run by au pair agencies, ten of them, and you agree with one of the agencies, in Utah, for you to work with them as your umbrella. Then you find au pairs, match them with families, pay the Utah agency a thousand dollars, get the J-1 visas, and bring in the au pairs. Right? Did I get that down pat?"

"Yes, but there's more."

"Was this what you were convicted of?"

"No, Dr. Marks, not even close! This has nothing to do with what the government charged me with, but everything to do with why I pissed off the government. Let me back up with some details. I didn't work alone in my office. I hired a young Irish woman to work alongside me. Her name was Mary, and she came to the U.S. on her own. She answered an ad in her hometown paper in Ireland; the ad had been posted by a U.S. couple seeking childcare. She flew to the U.S. and worked for them maybe two to three months before she quit and found me. Yes, she found me. She was a real live wire, had a lot of spirit. I thought she'd be an asset, so I hired her. She answered phones, made placements, and interviewed families with me. She was around thirty at the time.

"I took her along with me to some of my least favorite placements. I remember I interviewed a family for an au pair where the woman of the family was pregnant and had two or three older children. I can't remember all the details, but I think I found her an au pair, and the au pair quit immediately and went back to Ireland. I ended up telling someone that she had lost the baby and that was why I couldn't make a refund, something along that line, and, of course, she had not lost the baby. It was one of my lowest points in life, but I was getting accustomed to low points. Low points in my life became my norm.

"During this time, Mary and I became close. She watched as I scrambled to make placements. And then along came Avery, a good-looking Irish man who started to work with our office. I knew Mary liked him. He was about her age. It was fun to watch them flirt."

"You know," Dr. Marks interrupted, "we're getting close to ending today, but keep going; I'll let you run over a little. I don't have another patient for an hour."

"Okay, so everything is running smoothly. I'm making money, the Utah agency is making money, but some of the families started pushing the envelope. An au pair is only allowed to work thirty-five hours per week. But some families needed them for forty hours or even more. They kept insisting. So, I called the Utah agency and asked what they do about this type of problem. They told me that on the contract with the parents, they put down thirty-five hours, but what the parents and the au pair agree upon is their business. So, in other words, the clients can lie about it. But I didn't."

"Didn't what, Janie?"

"I didn't lie about it. I put down forty hours on the contract. I'm not sure why, but I did. I mean, the au pair was working maybe fifty hours per week. She was typically treated like an indentured slave. She made meals, did laundry, cleaned the house, and hell, she probably had to give the father a blow job every night. They worked them into the ground. Not everyone, but most.

"When Christmas came that year, all hell broke loose. I went to Missouri to see my parents, took my children, and was taking some much-needed time off. It was two days before Christmas when I got a call from the head supervisor of the au pair company in Utah, a woman, I don't remember her name. She told me nanny agencies reached out to some muckety mucks in the government and complained about the umbrella arrangement I had with the Utah agency. The government was insisting that the Utah agency break its relationship with me. I don't even know if they knew about the others. In addition to that, she had seen some contracts with the forty hours listed, and she couldn't possibly let the government see those. The woman begged me to write a letter 'to whom it may concern,' basically saying I went rogue, that I alone put the forty hours in the contact against the Utah agency's advice, basically that the Utah agency was innocent in everything. Then she told me that writing this letter was the only way they would keep working with, but we had to keep the forty hours off the contract."

"And?"

"And, yes, I wrote the letter. I'm so stupid. I had my back up against the wall financially. I was making lots of money with these au pairs and panicked at the thought of losing the visas. So, yes, I wrote the letter. I wrote it on Christmas Eve and faxed it to them before the close of business that day."

"Janie, were you still seeing your psychiatrist and taking an antidepressant?"

"Yes, but as I said, he added Prozac to the mix. Now, I was on two antidepressants."

"Talk about adding fuel to a burning fire, Janie. I can't believe this. He couldn't see you were manic?"

"I only had a half-hour visit with him every other month. How could he have picked that up? After a month of taking both antidepressants, I began to fly off the radar. I began to feel like Superwoman. You know, 'Look up in the sky, it's Superwoman.' Everyone around me kept telling me I was changing. I couldn't see it or feel it. Hey, I was happy, really, really happy."

"Sorry to do this, but we're out of time. Now don't run off and go off the grid. You have me interested."

"Oh, now I've got you interested. I thought shrinks had to be interested in all their patients."

"We are, we are. Now get going," he said with a furtive smile.

CHAPTER 12

TO TRULY UNDERSTAND WHAT I was going through, it's necessary to know something about my business. While lucrative, it wasn't easy. Dealing with parents seeking care for their children couldn't be. And it wasn't just the parents, it was the nannies too. Lots of pressure from both sides of the equation. The au pairs I worked with were young, mostly inexperienced, and with the girls from overseas, they were coming to a strange land a long, long way from home. Most of the foreign au pairs were sweet young women who had visions of living on "Southfork" in Dallas. They watched TV and figured all Americans lived like that.

Some of the au pairs told me they wanted to come to the U.S. to experience our culture. Actually, that was one of the fundamental ideas behind the government au pair program. But like their American counterparts, once they arrived and the families laid out what was expected, these young women felt overwhelmed. Not every au pair felt this way, but I can honestly say close to ninety percent of them did.

Most American families that I had made placements with had a long list of duties they expected. Typically, a family asked that the nanny take care of the children starting at seven am and watch over them until the parents arrived home, usually after six pm. The au pair was to make breakfast and lunch and then help prepare dinner. The au pair was to do the children's laundry, keep the children's rooms orderly and do 'light' housework.

And when I say 'light' housework, it includes vacuuming, dusting, and doing the dishes. So, the au pair was to look after the children from seven am to six pm, chase after the children, do the meals, and clean the house. I, myself, was a mother of three, and I couldn't find the time or energy to do what these families were asking from their au pairs. Watching children is exhausting enough without throwing in housework. The au pair would have had to drink Red Bull from sunrise to sunset. And then on top of that, the families expected the au pairs to participate in preparing dinner and cleaning up. So, in essence, their day didn't end until around seven pm. The young women I brought here from other countries, and in fact, U.S. nannies, too, found this daunting. They were shocked the families expected so much. So, these girls would call me and complain, and complain they did, in volumes. Watch the children, make meals, clean clothes, clean rooms and keep the house clean. The U.S. families were too demanding of these young women. Essentially, the families wanted slaves!

Many American families I worked with even wanted the au pair to help put the children to sleep in the evening. These families had the ill-conceived notion that the au pair loved the children and wanted to be a part of the family. Yes, usually, they did want to be part of the family but didn't want to *be* the family. Many times, I had to explain to the parents that the young woman enjoyed the children, but that they were nonetheless NOT the au pair's own children, that she wanted a life outside the family, a life that included people her own age; that she didn't want to sit and watch reruns of *Golden Girls* all night with her employers.

Some of these au pairs met families, were hired, and then quit by the end of the week. They would get on the first plane back to their own country. Not only could they not meet all the demands of the families, but they were homesick and racking up costly phone bills. Au pairs were only paid $100 per week, and sometimes their phone bills exceeded their pay. As for American nannies, they also knew there was a better life for them. A lot of them preferred to work in fast food or retail, while many also attended college.

I had one case where an au pair came to America on a Monday, and by Thursday, she called a taxi and escaped through the bathroom window with her suitcase. Another au pair faked a medical condition in order to be taken to the airport so she could go home. And when these things would happen, the families called me. They wanted a refund, or they instantly demanded another au pair. In some cases, they were hostile and threatened to "close me down." When I tried to explain that their demands were unrealistic, they ignored me.

Once, a single physician, a father of two, requested an au pair. He worked different shifts at a hospital and needed someone who could work flexible hours. I worked with him for two weeks, until he finally decided on a particular au pair. At the time, my data sheets on the au pairs did not come with a snapshot of each woman. The family would go over her resume and job qualifications, and then once they selected someone, they would do a telephone interview.

The physician did just that. He narrowed it down to one and then extended her an offer, which she enthusiastically accepted. He and his two children went to the airport to pick her up and take her home. Once they arrived, he went into his study and made a frantic phone call to me. His problem was that she was "too fat." He wanted a young slim woman, a woman he could use to make his ex-wife jealous. He told me that her size was an embarrassment to him, and so he demanded a refund or another au pair by the following week. So, what was I going to tell this naive young woman who came over from a foreign country? It was very difficult. I ended up lying to her and telling her he no longer needed an au pair because he was going to put his children in daycare.

She didn't buy it and asked me if he didn't want her because she was overweight. I hated my job at that moment.

Over my years in au pair placement, I have found that a situation works best when the job consists of only taking care of the children, and when the nanny is paid a fair salary with health benefits. When I conducted the placement of American nannies, sometimes the families would try to negotiate the salary. They had no problem with a huge mortgage but wanted to negotiate the lowest salary they could get away with for the caretaker of their children.

Suffice it say, it wasn't an easy job. But I was Superwoman. I was up to the task. Nothing was going to stand in my way—unfortunately.

CHAPTER 13

I DISTINCTLY REMEMBER THAT night. How could I possibly forget? The halfway house's night watch person, the woman who stayed overnight at the front desk, shook me, telling me to wake up. I was startled and asked what was wrong. I thought the place was on fire.

"Get up," she kept saying, "you have an urgent phone call downstairs." It had to be urgent because they would never wake you for a personal call. Hell, they wouldn't even take a message for a personal call, so I knew this was serious. Everything was rushing through my head at once. Did someone get hurt? Are my children Okay? My dad had heart problems. Is he Okay? I hurried down the four flights to the ground floor.

I grabbed the phone. It was my husband. My brother had a heart attack and was on life support at University Hospital in Baltimore. He said they didn't think he would live, and he asked me if I could get down there immediately.

I hung up the phone in disbelief. I had just been at the hospital to see him the day before. He had a blood disorder from a liver condition, and last week he started to hemorrhage. His liver was compromised even though he didn't drink. They talked about putting a stent in, but when I left him, he was fine. In fact, he was better than fine. He was laughing and joking around. He even asked me to run some errands for him, something for his new house.

The night monitor told me I could leave. It was 1:25 a.m. I changed clothes, grabbed my purse, and walked out the front door towards my parked car several blocks down. The streets of Georgetown were dimly lit. I felt I was in danger walking down that dark city street so early in the morning. It was fall, and the leaves were rustling in the trees. It reminded me of the scene in *To Kill a Mockingbird* where Scout and her brother walked through the woods after a Halloween play. I was waiting for someone to jump out and nab me, only Boo Radley would not be there to save the day.

I finally saw my car in the distance and made a sprint for it. I fumbled with my keys. Once I opened my car door, I slammed down the locks and started the ignition. I hoped my brother would be alive when I got to the hospital.

CHAPTER 14

"HEY, JANIE," DR. MARKS began with a sense of urgency, "I've got the popcorn popping. I'm ready to hear more."

"Really? You have popcorn?"

"Kidding, Janie. You're the last one I would have thought was gullible."

"I'm not on my game today, Dr. Marks. I have some terrible news. My brother is in the hospital on life support. I'm totally devastated."

"Would you like to skip today? Would it help to talk about your brother?"

"No," I said softly. "I'd like to get my mind off it."

"Then, please, go ahead, but let me know if you'd rather stop."

"Where was I? Oh, the Utah agency at Christmas when I sent them that stupid letter saying it was all my fault. When I got back from Missouri with the kids, the agency faxed me a letter stating that they could no longer do business with me because I was not following government rules. Ha! They wanted me to 'wink, wink' at the parents about the hours, then reassured me our relationship would continue, and that the *only* way we could was if I wrote that letter. But once the letter was in hand, they dropped me. I was duped."

"What did you expect, Janie? I mean, as they say, 'Get in bed with dogs, you're going to get fleas.' Why would you have expected anything different?"

"Because I was an idiot! Because I was grandiose! Because I spent more than I was bringing in and was in real financial trouble! Because! Because! Because! I don't know. I really don't know. I was outraged. Now looking back, as you said, they were corrupt; I had no right to be angry. I knew they were dirty and then got mad when they dirty-handed me. Yeah, I caught some fleas alright, and some big-ass flea bites at that."

"What next?"

"I called the government department that ran the au pair program and asked if I could become a sanctioned agency. I told them I knew how to recruit au pairs, that I had been doing it for ten months, maybe longer, and knew how to recruit families. But I was turned down flat. They told me they only needed ten agencies and were not willing at that point to expand. I told them that the agencies were probably doing what the Utah agency was doing, that they had other people recruiting under their umbrella, so why not open up the au pair market to all of us? And you know what they said?"

"Janie, don't make me guess."

"They told me that what I was telling them about other people working under an agency umbrella wasn't happening. In other words, what I had done with the Utah Company didn't happen."

"Must have been very frustrating. So, tell me what was going on in your personal life. You were manic, out of control, and you were in financial trouble. Not a good mix."

"I was spending money like wildfire. Every credit card I had was nearly maxed out. When I went shopping, I would buy not one, but two of everything. 'Wow, these shoes look good, can I get two pairs, please?' I was staying up all night, starting home projects and never finishing them. Sending my kids off to their grandparents' house, never really spending time with them. And my sexual desires were off the chart. I became promiscuous."

"Go on."

"I started an affair with my old druggie boyfriend, who, by the way, was married at the time. And what bothers me about it, looking back, was that I didn't feel bad. Not one ounce of guilt. This crazy life I was living seemed normal to me. When anyone would question me about it, I would think they were the crazy ones. Couldn't they see I was just enjoying life? Honestly, that's how I looked at things at the time."

"Didn't your husband question you about the credit cards and the hours you were keeping? Didn't he suspect you were having an affair?"

"He always let me run the finances in the family, so he didn't know about the credit cards until it was too late. He would question me about the hours and my odd behavior, even suspected I was having an affair, but I would always reassure him everything was Okay. He wanted to believe that, so he did.

"One morning I woke up and wondered what a San Francisco sunset was like. So, I picked up the phone and booked a flight, made reservations at a hotel, and was there in San Francisco to watch the sunset. Crazy? Don't even answer that. I went to a jazz club. When I left the club, I was walking up a hill to catch a cab when a homeless, drunk man approached me and asked for some change. I looked at him and said, 'I'll tell you what. I have cash in my purse, and I'm going to make it your grab bag. I'm going to open it up, and whatever bill you pull out, you get to keep. But you can only take one bill. He reached in and pulled out a $50 bill. I smiled at him and said, 'Looks like this is your lucky day.' Then I continued walking up the hill to catch a cab. He could have knocked me on my ass and snatched the purse; anything could have happened. I was a mother of three children wandering around a strange city, getting drunk, letting homeless men reach into my purse... what was I thinking?"

"Janie, you were manic. As you said, it all seemed normal to you. It was living on the edge. That's what manics do. They live on the edge and crave excitement. Nothing is too big, everything has to be exciting, and that night in San Francisco, it was exciting. And as a manic, you probably didn't feel impending danger."

"Let me tell you what I didn't feel. No shame or guilt; I had no moral compass. I was literally running with the devil. Everything I said was a lie, shady, or the product of ulterior motives. The crazy life was intoxicating. Fucking intoxicating. The more dangerous or wrong it was, the more exciting it was. I felt that I could sit down with world leaders and solve the world's problems. I was faster than a speeding bullet, more powerful than a locomotive, able to leap tall buildings in a single bound. Look up in the sky, it's Super Janie!"

"Like most manics, you were living in the moment, looking for instant gratification."

"Let me tell you about instant gratification. When I was a little girl, around ten years old or so, I was in a car with my mother, my brother, and my cousin David. My mother had given us all Hershey chocolate kisses in clear baggies. She told us we could eat them all now or wait until after dinner, and if we didn't eat them right away, she would give us more for waiting. Well, the boys were in the backseat, and they gobbled theirs up right away. I was in the front seat with my mother, and she kept praising me over and over for having the patience to wait. The boys were in the back seat just laughing. I sat smugly in the front seat, just basking in the praise from my mom. An hour later, we reached our destination, and I reached down to retrieve my bag of Hershey Kisses. I held the bag up and saw they had all melted. When the boys saw this, they laughed hysterically. My mom told me she was so sorry. I can still hear them laughing at me. And what did I learn from all this? The boys were right after all. If you pass up the chance for instant gratification, it might just melt away."

"Understandable that you could feel that way. Let's stay on track. Tell me more about your manic days."

"Every fucking night was Mardi Gras! That's how I felt."

"Still on the cocktail of antidepressants?"

I just nodded my head in agreement. "I remember, Dr. Marks, one particular evening when I was quite manic, I watched TV way into the morning. Somehow, I found myself on QVC, the shopping network. Now, normally I didn't bother with QVC because you had to order things and then wait for delivery a week later. When you're manic, you can't bear the thought of having to wait for anything. Instant gratification.

"Well, that evening I was enthralled with everything they were selling. I wanted to buy everything, so I damn nearly did. My eyes were glazed over from no sleep, and I had my debit card out. When the announcer would say, 'Only twenty more left. You better put in your order before we sell out.' Boom, I would be on the phone ordering it. When it was all said and done, I probably spent close to five hundred dollars. Five hundred dollars I couldn't spare.

"A week later when the items started to come, I didn't even know what was in the packages. I had ordered so much that I lost track, and, of course, like the manic I was, I explained it away in my mind. I gave myself a pass each and every time. There was no accountability."

"Okay, Janie, your personal life is in shambles, and you're dumped by the Utah agency. What was next?"

"Lawsuits began to pile up. When the Utah agency cut me off, there were five families who had already paid me for au pairs. I had to figure out a way to deliver."

"Why didn't you just refund their money?"

I laughed hard at that one. I looked at Dr. Marks and said, "Are you kidding me? I already spent the money, all of it, as soon as it came in. I had a staff of two, and they had to be paid, and the rest I spent, crazy spending, no-rhyme-or-reason spending. 'Oh, there's a tree house for my son, seven hundred dollars. I'll pull my car over on the side of the road and buy it.' That kind of spending. Upside down, crazy, over-the-top spending. Give them a refund?

"Then, my husband finds out about the affair, and his move was to leave and take the kids. I'm alone in a huge house with a huge mortgage, no money at all, from any source. I was desperate. The kids would come over to visit, and I would have to borrow money from my parents just to buy food for them. I did have my parents, and they were a comfort. I had my in-laws, and they were also a comfort. Then, my parents decided it was time to move to Missouri to retire. And if that wasn't a jolt, a week later my in-laws decided to move to California to be near their oldest son and his sons. Within one month, they were all gone. All my back-up people, all the people I loved, my support system, they were gone. My husband gone, my parents gone, and my in-laws gone. But you know what?"

"I'm not good at guessing, Janie."

"Everyone's gone, right? I felt excitement. That's right, I was upset that they had left, but my veins were pumping excitement. I still wanted to continue my affair; still, spend what little money I had. I was still full of excitement. And every time I saw my psychiatrist who was prescribing the antidepressants that were keeping me high, I would lie my ass off and tell him I was doing just fine. But, you know, maybe I wasn't lying. I didn't actually know why I felt that excited. I hadn't exactly connected the dots. But I knew if I had told him about all the events in my life, he might have wanted to adjust the medication, and I didn't want that. Not only did I not want to lose the high, but I didn't want to take the chance of being depressed again.

"I wish, and wishing is all I can do now, that my family had been aware of my problem, and that they would have taken note of my behavior and contacted my psychiatrist. But, remember, my mother and father didn't believe in psychiatry and, therefore, I wasn't or couldn't be mentally ill. My husband buried his head in the sand. He understood depression, even dragged my ass to the psychiatrist, but he didn't understand the monster called 'mania.' So, I was left to my own devices, which destroyed me in the end."

"Janie, let's not be overly dramatic. You weren't destroyed by the 'Terminator.' You're sitting here quite lucid and looking good. I think by your parents leaving, your husband leaving, your in-laws leaving, it made for the perfect storm. You had to be feeling desperate, even in your mania. So, how did you handle it? What did you do, Janie Renee?"

"I tried to game the system. I knew au pairs could come over on student visas. The problem was I didn't have any schools working with me. I met with some technical schools that said they would enroll the au pairs, but they couldn't offer up any student visas until the au pairs got here. I called the au pairs and told them to just say at Customs that they were here on tourist visas. I figured, as crazy as it sounds now, that once they got here, I could get them student visas."

"None of the au pairs objected?"

"Some did, but out of the seven I brought over, most didn't. One poor girl got off the plane after an eight-hour flight and Customs became suspicious and detained her. She gave them my name and number. They released her but made her get back on a plane and go back to Ireland. I know now that must have scared her to death, to be detained and questioned. I now feel so bad about that."

"Janie, what did you think would happen to you if the government found out? Were you aware that you were breaking the law?"

"I thought, mind you, it would only be a handful of au pairs I would do this with. I thought if I got caught, they would fine me. That's it, just fine me. Mary started helping me find au pairs in Ireland and stayed by my side during those rough times. But, to answer your question, yes, I did know I was breaking the law. Let me try to explain this.

I knew what I was doing was illegal, but in my mind, the crime seemed so petty to me, and I didn't feel any consequences would come my way. I was manic. There would not be any consequences.

"Then, the young Irish man I had hired, Avery, started paying a lot of attention to me. He was a very good-looking boy, around twenty-seven; he had jet-black hair, bright blue eyes, a strong chin, and a small nose. His hair was thick, and he oozed sex appeal. When he sat next to me, I could feel the chemistry. Mary took notice. She didn't like it, not one bit. As Avery would sit in the office and lean into me while talking, I could see Mary on the other side of the room staring at us with disdain. One day I broached the subject with Mary. She told me she didn't care who Avery was interested in. I knew that wasn't true, that she was feeling the sting of rejection and was upset.

"Had I been thinking straight, and I've already made it clear I wasn't, I would have backed away. I was already having an affair with a married man while I was married to Mike and was now sleeping with a twenty-seven-year-old. It was exciting and totally manic. I was in my own world and thought the world revolved around me."

"Janie, since you were manic, you couldn't have thought this out. You weren't able to see the consequences of your actions. That's not how mania works. But I'm confused about something. I thought you and Mike had separated?"

"No, that didn't happen until all this went down. We separated, got back together, separated again; it's very hard to keep up with it all. We were always back and forth. I was also feeling that any action I took would always work out in the end. I kept going back to feeling invincible; I don't know any other way to explain it. My mom liked to say I was in 'La-La Land.' Maybe that explains it better."

"Hey, Janie, you wouldn't be the first one I know who visited La-La Land. Some people I know still live there. And just where do you think La-La Land is, Janie?"

"Somewhere over the rainbow?"

"No, Janie, that's Oz."

"Then hell if I know. La-La Land might be a nice place to visit, but you don't want to live there, trust me."

CHAPTER 15

WHEN I GOT TO the hospital, Terry was alive, barely. He was lying on his back, bloated and swollen. I was told that after I left the hospital the day I had gone to see him, he started to bleed from his eyes, nose, and mouth. They rushed him by ambulance to University Hospital, and while on the way, he suffered a heart attack and was without oxygen for 20 minutes. Would he be brain dead?

I sat in the hospital for most of the day. My mother had flown in from Missouri a couple of days earlier just for a visit. She had no idea her son would be dying a couple of days later; she was in total shock. Terry's wife was comforted by her brother and relatives, and my mom and I just sat holding hands.

The doctor in charge came in to see us. On a scale of one to ten, one being the worst, he was sorry to tell us that Terry was a one. We all looked at each other. The doctor looked down at his notes and then back at us. He rested his eyes on my mother, saying, "I'm sorry." We knew then Terry wouldn't make it.

I had to return to the halfway house that evening without knowing if my brother would live through the night. When I got into bed that evening, my roommates comforted me, but I could hardly be consoled. The following morning, I jumped out of bed, dressed, and headed to my home where my mom was staying. When I arrived, I saw a neighbor who had been called by my husband to take care of our children. Mom was ready to go, and we were heading out the door when the call came in.

It was my husband. He said in a light, sad voice, "He's gone, Janie." I put the phone down lightly and looked into my mother's eyes. She was searching my face for hope. She grabbed one of my arms and said, "Tell me, tell me what he said."

I looked over at her. "He's gone." She burst into tears and ran to the car. I ran after her pleading with her to slow down. I asked her where she wanted to go. She wanted to be taken to the hospital to see him.

There was dead silence between us as we drove to Baltimore. My heart was pounding. She kept a fixed stare on the road. She wasn't crying any longer and seemed to be in a trance. I looked over at her when I came to a stop light and asked her if she was good. She didn't turn to me; she simply replied with one terse, "No!"

It was raining that day, and as I drove through the streets of Baltimore, I took notice of all the construction, the wrecking balls, jackhammers, and crews. I thought how Terry will never get to a construction site again. I could see the hotdog vendors on the street corners, thinking he would never smell those smells again. He dearly loved hotdogs.

When I reached the hospital, I asked my mother if she wanted me to let her out at the entrance, and I would go park the car. She shook her head no, and replied, "I need you with me when I see him." We parked the car, and as we walked to the hospital there were homeless people asking for money. Mom seemed oblivious to all the noise and all the people. She was focused on getting into the front door of the hospital.

When the elevator door opened, she walked out as if on a mission. She knew exactly where she was going, which room he was in. We walked in. He was lying there on his back with the sheets pulled up to his chin. It was very quiet. My mom went to his right, and I went to his left. She picked up one of his hands, and I picked up the other. She leaned down and said, "You were my first born, and I will always love you. You will never leave my heart. I love you, Terry." And then she let out all her pent-up emotions and wept.

I looked down at my brother in disbelief. He couldn't be dead, no way. I was holding a warm hand. He looked alive to me, just sleeping. I wanted to shake him and demand he quit playing this joke and wake up. I let out a sigh. It was over. He was gone, and I would just have to come to terms with that. The thought of that exhausted me. I suddenly became overwhelmingly sleepy. My emotions were scrambling all over. My mind was processing thoughts and feelings at such a rapid pace. I just wanted it to shut down and let me sleep.

I took my mom by the elbow and told her it was time to go.

"No, it isn't," she insisted. "He needs me here."

"No, Mom, he doesn't," I replied. "He needs to be left alone so everyone else can come in and say goodbye."

We left the hospital that day the same way we entered, in silence. We walked by the homeless people, the street vendors selling their hot-dogs, and the construction crews. While the sounds of the city were there, we didn't hear them.

I drove my mom home, and we both went to bed. I slept for twelve straight hours. Mom didn't sleep a wink. We were processing our grief in very different ways.

It was time to prepare for the funeral and head to Missouri where Terry would be laid to rest.

CHAPTER 16

"DR. MARKS, HE DIED... he's gone."

"Oh, I'm so sorry, Janie. When?"

"Yesterday."

"We don't have to do our session today. In fact, it's better if we don't."

I didn't say anything for the longest time. Dr. Marks didn't either. Finally, he broke the silence.

"Where will the funeral be?"

"In Missouri."

"Are you allowed to go?"

"Actually, I need special permission from the Bureau of Prisons."

"What can I do to help you facilitate that?"

"I'm not sure."

"Well, let me know, and I'll help."

"Dr. Marks, I'd like to have our session if that's Okay? I don't want to go home and watch Mom cry and sit there feeling so helpless. I want to comfort her, but it's like she's off in another dimension. She cries and just stares into space. Nothing cheers her up, no matter what I try. It's so pitiful."

"It's grief, raw grief, Janie. She knows you're there, and if she needs you, she'll come to you. Do you want to talk more about your brother today?"

"No, not today. I'm still in denial. If I talk about it, it will seem real to me. And I don't want that. I want to stay in denial, just for a little while."

"Fine. Why don't you tell me what you did after the young au pair was sent home, the one Customs put on a plane to go back as soon as she arrived. At that time, you must have thought the jig was up?"

"No, actually, I didn't. I kept trying to bring them over. I was out of my friggin' mind! I'm rolling along, carrying on an affair, had no money to pay my mortgage, but as I said, wasn't even worried about it. Saw my kids four times a week, and that was just fine with me. I don't even like talking about it. Can you imagine how screwed up they felt? Their lives were upside down, and there I was, acting like life was normal. I'm surprised they didn't end up at a clock tower somewhere shooting at people with a high-powered rifle. But it all must have seemed normal to them too in some way. Hell, even I didn't know exactly how much trouble I was in until one day I get a knock on the door. Standing there was a young reporter from *The Washington Post*, David Montgomery. He told me he wouldn't take up much of my time, but wanted to know if I'd like to comment on the charges pending against me."

"What charges, Janie?"

"That was my question exactly. Hell, if I knew! So, I asked him. He told me the United States Attorney was putting together charges against me for immigration fraud. He said I got on the government's radar when the department that oversaw au pairs thought I was operating an illegal service. When they investigated, they found the lawsuits against me from families who didn't get their au pairs. The government called and talked to them. They told them exactly what I had done. In some cases, the families got an au pair on a tourist visa and in others, they didn't get an au pair at all even though they paid me. The dominoes started to fall. The young reporter standing in front of me wanted to know if I had a comment."

"Did you?" Dr. Marks asked.

"'No, Mr. Washington Post,' I said to him. 'I don't have a comment.' He put away his notebook and told me off the record that I pissed off the wrong people. I asked him who the right people to piss off would be. He laughed and told me that the people who filed complaints had money and influence. He was, of course, talking about my clients. It was no surprise that they had enough influence to get immediate attention, especially since they were right. He told me they were demanding my head on a silver platter. I asked him if a public flogging would suffice. He smiled and said he doubted it, that they probably wanted me in prison.

"'Prison?' I shouted, 'Fucking prison? For seven illegal nannies? No way does someone go to prison for seven illegal nannies.' He took his notebook back out and opened it. 'We'll see. Now would you like to comment?'"

"What did you say?"

"Well, I looked this young reporter up and down. Who had sent this young whippersnapper to my door? I thought it must have been a slow day at *The Washington Post* to be getting involved with a housewife who committed a minor crime. A small crime in my mind. I was thinking of how they must have drawn straws to see who would be forced to go out and cover this meaningless story. Poor David Montgomery must have drawn the short straw. So, I told him I was screwed. He took it down."

"How were you feeling after he left?"

"I still had that same excited feeling. Nothing would come of it. I was invincible. That night, I went out with my boyfriend and continued to spend money that my husband was now paying me. Not enough money to pay the mortgage, but enough to eat. I even spent the bill money."

"Janie, let me stop you here and put some things in perspective." He paged through his file. "I see here, in 1982, you were the county's 'Businesswoman of the Year.'"

I nodded.

He flipped to the next page. "Then you worked for a lobbyist for six years, worked for a computer school as a placement director, bought a condo, sold it, then you and your husband bought an expensive house, attended church, helped your in-laws with their bills in their time of need, had friends that you and your husband socialized with. Is that right?"

"Yes, so what's your point?"

"Well, a short time later, you were living on the edge, flying to San Francisco, having affairs. Could you not see the distinct contrast between how you had lived your life before and how you were living it then?"

"I don't get it. How many times have you said you understood that I couldn't get it because I was manic?"

"I did, and I'm not being judgmental. I'm just trying to understand if at any time did you feel the contrast between where you had come from and where you wound up?"

"Well, yes, at times I did see the difference but thought I needed the excitement to live fully. I would look at my old life and think it was boring. I didn't like the troubles I was encountering but always thought everything would work out in the end. I never, ever thought of the consequences."

"And now, Janie, looking back at the life you had with your husband, how do you feel?"

"They were the happiest days of my life. I would sell my soul to the devil to relive one year of that life. Or maybe I already sold my soul to the devil and that's why I have all these mental problems."

"A little over dramatic, don't you think? You know, that's a problem for manics. When they're well, they suffer the consequences that they never felt at the time."

"I guess I could say, 'That's just how it goes.' But I'm talking about my life. My life, damn it. Mental illness had a grip on me. I may not have been well, but thought I was at the top of my game. Shit, mania kicked my fucking ass. I was down for the count and didn't even know it."

"Janie, I'm sorry that your psychiatrist didn't see it or that your family wasn't able to get you to see you needed help. Now, it's time to be good to yourself. I'd like to focus on that next time."

"You know, Dr. Marks before it got better my life got even more bizarre."

"Hold that thought, Janie Renee."

I got up and started to walk out of the office. As I got to the door, I turned around and said, "I saw my brother Sunday. We joked and laughed. Forty-eight hours later he's dead."

"I'm sure you're still in disbelief, in shock."

"I'm numb. My mom is still staying with me but has to get back to my dad who didn't come up because of his poor health. He's taking it so hard he can barely talk on the phone. The funeral will be in Missouri, so I'm hoping that won't be a problem with the feds."

"As I said, I don't know how that works, Janie, but I'll put in a good word if you like."

"I loved him," Dr. Marks. "He was not just my brother. We became friends. He lived a life that others preached about. He talked the talk and walked the walk. I don't see that often."

"I don't either, Janie."

"His daughter is only nine. His oldest sons are in their twenties. He'll never get to know his grandchildren. But Terry was a Christian. He believed in heaven and always told me he didn't fear death. He had a calm demeanor about him, an inner peace."

"Janie, please, sit. Let me tell my next patient I'll be a few minutes." I sat down. A minute later, he was back.

"A lot of times," I continued, "when someone dies, people say things like, 'He's at peace now.' Thing is, Dr. Marks, he was already at peace.

Terry believed that Jesus died for our sins; he put his trust in Him. Terry had a good life and according to his belief, he has a better one now. I want to believe that. I get a peaceful feeling believing that.

"I remember one time, Terry and I were in a restaurant, and I was going on and on about an unhappy relationship I was in at the time. Terry kept shushing me, but I just got louder and louder. Someone behind us asked me to tone it down and be quiet, but instead, I got even louder. Terry shook his head and begged me not to get him into a fight."

"Were you manic at the time, Janie?"

"Every time I stand up for something, everyone jumps to the 'Are you manic?' Could it be that I was just passionate about something?"

"Yes, Janie, it could, but getting thrown out of bars, getting arrested on immigration charges, going to prison, that goes beyond passion. Your passion defeats you."

"Then let it defeat me."

"I'm afraid, Janie, that today you might feel defeated because you lost someone you loved very much."

I started to cry. Dr. Marks put his hand on my shoulder. I began to feel the first signs of loss and grief. It finally hit me.

❖ ❖ ❖

The day after Terry died, a year after he bailed me out of jail, I asked my counselor to put in a request for me to go out of state to Missouri for the funeral. That evening the counselor called me into his office and told me that my trip had been authorized with certain stipulations. I had to fly, not travel by car, train, or bus. When I got to Missouri I had to report to the federal marshals in the nearest town, and if the local marshals wanted to attend the funeral, I could not refuse. I was given only three days. I immediately agreed to the terms, but I couldn't quite understand why in the world a federal marshal would want to attend my brother's funeral. Later, someone explained that if I seemed to them to be a flight risk, they had a right to maintain twenty-four-hour surveillance. A flight risk? I couldn't get away long enough to get my hair done without one of the kids demanding I take him with me, or worse, buy him something while we were out. All the federal marshals really had to do was to pay my kids to do what they did naturally, watch me.

The day of the funeral I drove my dad to the funeral home early so he could spend an hour with Terry before the service began. Terry was laid out in his casket at the front. I took a seat in the back. My father slowly went over to Terry. It had been a long time since my dad saw him. I watch as my ailing father bent his body over the casket so his head could rest on Terry's chest. I could hear his cries from the back pew.

The funeral home was one of the oldest in town. It hadn't been renovated in 50 years. The floors were warped, and creaked as I walked; the old floorboards were moving underneath the worn carpet. The curtains were a heavy fabric and pulled tightly closed. The overwhelming smell of air freshener hung over the stale room.

My father spent an entire hour with his frail frame bent over the casket, his head on his son's chest. People began to form a line outside. It was time to get my dad to a seat. I walked up to him on the creaky floor and tugged on his elbow. He didn't flinch. I tugged harder. He broke down and wailed. He finally stood up. He looked at me with his swollen eyes and asked me where he was supposed to sit. I took him to his seat and then let everyone in.

The funeral was nice, I guess as nice as a funeral can be. My parents looked so sad and alone as they sat in the front pew of the vigil room and greeted everyone. My mom would at times get up and look at the flowers and chat with people, but my dad never moved. He sat in one spot, staring at Terry in his casket.

I found myself as the go-between for my parents and the many well-wishers who attended. Everyone, of course, asks what they can do for you. It's a polite thing to ask that society has taught us, but honestly, as anyone knows who has buried a loved one, there is nothing anyone can do. The grieving process takes time, and I knew it would take a lot of time for my parents. Their only daughter was living in a federal halfway house and now their only son had died. What else could they bear? My dad was only sixty-eight, but on that day he looked ninety.

Sometimes a funeral can be a circus. Raw emotions are a breeding ground for discontent and arguments. Our family was no exception. I don't know why I argued with some of the people I saw during those three days, but I did. My mother was upset with things, my aunts were upset over things, and everyone said they wanted peace, but it was nowhere to be found. Terry's funeral had brought out the worst in many of us. I was glad when my three days were up and happy to get on the plane, which would take me back to normalcy. I never would have believed that going back to a federal halfway house was normalcy. Never would have believed it.

CHAPTER 17

"JANIE, ARE YOU READY to talk about your brother today?"

"No, Dr. Marks. If you don't mind."

"Of course not. You begin then. Wherever you'd like."

"Well, I finally knew I had to get a lawyer. The problem was I didn't have any money. I went to my estranged husband and put myself at his mercy. Luckily, he got a lawyer for me. He and the lawyer worked out a payment plan. I felt a huge burden lifted. I found the lawyer from a referral by a former classmate from high school.

"The day I first met him, he was wearing bright-red suspenders, sitting behind his desk, pushing around a lot of papers. He looked up at me when I walked in and said, 'What the hell was in the water at your high school? You're the third person from your graduating class I've represented. What were you all smoking that year?' He asked me about *The Washington Post* and advised me sternly not to give interviews to anyone. 'Keep your mouth shut, Janie, and I know that's hard,' is what he advised me that day. He was very strong on this point. I agreed. We talked about him getting in touch with the prosecutor's office and finding out what dirt they had on me. Before I left, he warned me again about not giving interviews.

"I also knew my business was over. I knew the jig was up the day that a reporter from *The Washington Post* came to my door. Just a day later, I was in the office sifting through paperwork when Mary came in, the young Irish girl who worked with me. She sat down on the couch, crossed her legs, and lit up a cigarette. She reached for an ashtray and began to ask me about Avery. I told her he had left for Ireland, and at once the shit hit the proverbial fan. I told her I was sorry if I had hurt her feelings for having had an affair with him. I meant it, Dr. Marks. At the moment, I felt some tinge of sorrow for her. I really didn't mean to hurt her feelings, or anyone else's. I was just living in my manic, self-centered sphere.

"Mary inhaled her cigarette, blew out the smoke, and then looked me squarely in the eye. 'I've opened up my own au pair service, Janie, and the government is going to let me run the operation on a legal basis.' I asked, 'And just how is that?'

"She uncrossed her legs, then re-crossed them, and said, 'Not only am I running my own agency, but I've been given immunity for everything I've done with you, and I don't have to return to Ireland; they're letting me stay here.'

"My head was swirling, and I could feel the knife go in my back ever so slowly. She was enjoying this. 'You know, I went to the government and turned you in. I told them what you were doing, all about the illegal au pairs. And, Janie, were they ever interested.' She leaned in closer and whispered, 'I hope Avery was worth it.' She put out her cigarette, grabbed her purse and stood up. 'You're going down, Janie, and I have a front-row seat.' And with that, she left. I knew then that a broken heart trumps loyalty. And with that, I got up and poured a glass of wine. I stared out the window, wondering what prison would feel like."

"What a sense of betrayal you must have felt."

"I went right to my lawyer's office. Actually, I didn't really like him, but he had a good reputation, and I had faith in him. I guess it didn't matter if I liked him or not. I just wanted him to untangle the mess I had gotten into. Three days later, a BBC crew was at my front door.

They were with a British show, the equivalent of our *60 Minutes*. This very nice, sweet, good-looking woman was standing on my porch saying things like, 'With all the charges against you, Mrs. Cochran, wouldn't you like to tell your story? We're here for you to tell your side.' I knew better, and I remembered what my lawyer had told me, but I invited her and her crew in, anyway. What a mistake.

"As soon as she came in with her crew, I told her I had to contact my lawyer to see if I could give the interview. But I knew what he would say, so I went against his advice and did it anyway. She was delighted. She sat down in a chair, had her crew wire me up, and before I knew it, the camera was rolling. This nice, sweet woman transformed before my eyes into a barracuda. She pounced on me with no mercy."

"How?"

"As soon as the cameras were rolling, she leaned toward me and asked, 'Why did you rip off all those families? And why did you keep those au pairs as hostages in your garage?'

"'What, what?' I kept asking. I couldn't believe it. 'What are you talking about? I never kept anyone hostage in my garage.' See, Dr. Marks, we converted our garage into a large playroom, and when the au pairs would suddenly leave families because they didn't want to do the job since they had no place to go, I would let them stay in the play-room on a fold-out couch. When the story broke, my home paper, *The Bowie Blade*, ran an article that claimed I held au pairs against their will in my garage. Anyway, Dr. Marks, this BBC reporter started to really pounce on me. It felt like I was at the Nuremberg trials. She said things like, 'Oh, you're saying they all lied, Ms. Cochran? Why would all these people lie? Do you have a conscience?'

"As the camera was rolling, she kept leaning into me and asking questions like, 'Why did you do it?' And, 'Why did you take all those people's money?' It was rapid-fire. I couldn't compose myself. I would hesitate for one second and think about what she had asked me, and there she was with another question. They say hookers are 'pros.' No way. I had met a pro that day in that interviewer; she defined 'pro.'

"What was going on in my mind at the time was scary. I thought for a second she was going to torture me to get answers. In today's terms, it would be like fearing she would waterboard me. I kept thinking, don't torture me, lady; I'll tell you anything you want to know.

"Dr. Marks, I wanted to give my side of the story, but she wasn't going to allow that. She had an agenda, and man, was she ever good at her job! I squirmed, sweated all throughout the interview, and finally, it was over. She took her wire off and then transformed back to the sweet woman I saw on my porch. She reached over and extended her hand and said, 'Thank you, Janie, for the interview.' Oh shit, I kept thinking, she screwed me. The interview was awful. I just incriminated myself. I asked her not to leave, to keep the cameras rolling so I could explain myself. She just smiled with her pretty, perfect white teeth and said, 'I think we have everything we need. You have a lovely home. Good day.'"

"Janie, why didn't you listen to your lawyer? That's why he was getting paid, to give you advice."

"Yes, I know, but in my frame of mind, I actually thought I would get a chance to explain myself. She hoodwinked me. I was stupid. I wanted my fifteen minutes of fame, dammit!"

"No, Janie, I wouldn't say you were stupid. You were frantic to set things straight. But given that chance in an open forum, what would you have said?"

"I don't know, I really don't know. I probably would have, in my manic state, just ranted. And you know what my biggest worry was at the time? I was worried if I would look fat on camera."

Dr. Marks laughed.

"Shortly after that interview, the U.S. Attorney's office contacted my lawyer and asked for a proffer session."

"I'm not quite sure what that is," Dr. Marks said.

"The prosecution meets with the intended defendant, and shows the accused the evidence they have in hopes of reaching some sort of plea deal."

"And you and your attorney went to this?"

"Oh, indeed we did. They showed me what evidence they had, which I already knew. They showed me the names of the women who were brought over illegally, the names of clients I had arranged for the au pairs to work for. After looking over their list, I put it down on the table, and the head prosecutor spoke up and said, 'We're not saying you won't do prison time, but if you admit to things now, we will work to see you get less time than you would if you go to trial.'

"I looked over at my attorney, and he sat in his chair expressionless. I could see then that this 'proffer session' was one big shit show. I asked to step out and speak to my attorney. Once we were in the hallway, I got panicky. I started asking him if they could actually put me in prison. And if so, for how long? He told me they could, but we could probably beat this with an insanity defense, that because I was out of control from the antidepressants, he thought he could beat this with a jury trial, that it would be like the 'Twinkie Defense.'"

"Wasn't that where a man, hyped up on sugar, committed a crime and was acquitted?"

"Exactly. Dr. Marks, I didn't know what to think. To tell you the truth…."

"Yes, please do, Janie," he said with a smile.

"Honestly, back then, I was just thinking about lunch. I was hungry. I just wanted lunch. Remember, I didn't think too long and hard over consequences. Yes, I got panicky when they mentioned prison, but that feeling subsided and the old feeling of excitement quickly replaced it. I told my lawyer I would not accept a plea deal, and that we could talk about the Twinkie Defense over lunch. We walked back into the room, and he said, 'No deal.' They weren't happy about it, and even told me

I was making a huge mistake. As I was leaving, the prosecutor looked at me and said, 'See you very soon, Janie.' It was very ominous, and it turned out to be so true. He was a man of his word. I'll say that for him."

"What next?"

"Mary showed up again one evening. I was in my office with two of my friends when there was a knock on the door. My friends cautioned me not to let her in, but being manic, there was no logic. I was curious about what she had to say. She sat down and told me she just wanted to clear the air on a few issues. 'Sure,' I told her, 'tell me exactly how you betrayed me.' She laughed and then threw her head back and started to ask questions that made little sense."

"Like what?"

"She brought up situations from the past where we worked together, and she kept trying to excuse her betrayal. Questions were just pouring out of her. Then it hit me. She was wired. I stood up and told her it was time to leave. She said, 'Remember, I have a front-row seat.' I never saw that treacherous bitch again. When she left the office, I wondered what made her so vindictive and mean. I knew she was unhappy with the way she looked. She was overweight and didn't have a lot of confidence. But that alone didn't make her who she was. She was bitter. and she was ugly on the inside. I almost felt sorry for her.

"Three months later, one morning, my nephew asked for a ride to work. I got up and kept on my flimsy nighty, figuring I wouldn't have to get out of the car, and so what the hell. We walked out the front door and that's when I saw two cars drive into my driveway, one blocking the other. Four people got out. 'Hi, Janie, today's the day,' one of them said. I knew what day they were talking about. They were federal marshals. I asked him if I could go back into the house and change my clothes. He told me, 'No.' He said I was going to the downtown Baltimore Federal Building to be arraigned, booked, and fingerprinted. He turned me around and slapped a pair of handcuffs on my wrists."

"Janie, you must have felt some regret then."

"Nope. Once again, just excitement. I knew the day was coming, but I was still on my cocktail of drugs so I couldn't feel anything but intense excitement. That's when they took me to McDonald's and got me an Egg McMuffin. They got me out of the car, and I just stood there in the parking lot, in my nightie, with no explanation."

"Did you feel humiliated?"

"No, actually. I realized after standing there for ten minutes that I was on public display. They wanted me to be humiliated, but, as you know, Dr. Marks, it's hard to humiliate someone who's manic. It just added to the excitement. And I was angry. They were pricks. And don't even bother telling me, 'It was their job.' They enjoyed every minute of it. They sent out four cars, which had been sitting in front of my house, as I was told by neighbors, since five a.m. They treated me as if I was the infamous "Unabomber". What a fuss over a first-time-offender house-wife who committed a non-violent crime. Four cars and six marshals? Please, already. Did they think I was David Koresh and would hold up in my house and refuse to come out? Maybe have a shootout?"

"I'm sure, Janie, it was just standard procedure. I wouldn't take it so personally."

"Wait until it happens to you and then tell me that."

"Please, go on."

"Eventually another federal marshal placed me in yet another back seat and off we went. When we reached the Federal Building in Balti-more, all six of them paraded me through the lobby in my sheer nighty. The building was air-conditioned, and I started shivering. They didn't care; they probably were amused. We caught the elevator, and did I ever get looks from the workers!

"They took me into a small office where a woman was sitting; she was the Arraignment Coordinator. She looked at me, looked at them, and said, 'You guys couldn't even let her put on some clothes?' They smiled, almost laughed. She ordered them to uncuff me, and they did, but I could tell they didn't want to. She went over what was going to happen that day and asked me who I wanted to call. I told her, my attorney.

"When we were finished, I was handcuffed again and taken to a jail cell. I was freezing and shivering. A federal marshal told me I would be seeing a judge in an hour or two. I asked him if he could get me a blanket or coat, and he told me that wasn't in his job description, but I could ask the people who supervised the jail. In the cell, there was one metal bed, a toilet, and a sink. Nothing else. One metal bed to sit on or lie down on, take your choice.

"I started yelling between the bars for someone to come and see me. A man showed up and asked me what I was yelling about. I stood there shivering and asked if he could find me a blanket or a coat. He told me he didn't have any blankets but would be happy to give me his jacket. So, he took off his jacket, opened the cell, and handed it to me. I lay down on the metal slab, covered up by that man's jacket, and fell asleep. I didn't wake up until the man who had given me his jacket woke me. My attorney had arrived. They took me into a small room. I could see the shock on my lawyer's face when he saw what I was wearing.

"He started asking me questions about the arrest, wanted to see if they read me my rights. He told me that I was going to have to make bail. I said, 'And just who am I going to get to do that? I'm not speaking with anyone in my family, or should I say, they're not speaking to me. Where am I going to get bail?' He looked at me, shoved his glasses up on his nose, and replied, 'Well, your brother Terry is here and so is your husband.' I was separated at the time and couldn't believe my husband had come. This was a year before Terry died.

"I asked my lawyer, 'How in the hell did you get a hold of my brother?' He told me that he called my soon-to-be ex-husband, who, in turn, called my brother, and both of them were waiting in the courtroom for me to be arraigned. At that moment, Dr. Marks, I finally felt something other than excitement. I felt gratitude, and I felt humbled. My brother, my only sibling, had left work to come to help me. He was an electrician and left his job to drive to Baltimore, just for me. I wanted to cry, I was so moved. And my husband, well, even though we were separated, he cared enough to come and bail me out. I also felt love, intense love."

"You said they were there in the courtroom?"

"Yes, they were waiting for me. It was about an hour after the meeting with my lawyer. I didn't have a real sense of time since there were no windows in the jail cell, and I wasn't wearing a watch. I figured it had to be somewhere in the afternoon. The marshals ushered me into court, handcuffed me and sat me in the front row. I looked over at my brother and my husband, and they both gave me the thumbs up. I smiled. I almost felt like laughing hysterically, I was so happy."

"It felt good to have loved ones there."

"Oh, God, yes! They didn't understand mania or why I had done what I did, but they weren't there to judge me or ask questions. They were there to support me and love me. Oh, if you only knew how beautiful that felt.

"So, my name is called, and I go before the judge; there I stood, handcuffed behind my back, wearing that pink nighty. The judge looked down from the bench, and in a rough voice, ordered the marshals to uncuff me. I started rubbing my wrists, and the marshals told me to take off the coat the jailer had given me. I don't know why they wanted that, but I took it off, exposing more of my body. I started to shiver once again, and just stood there while the judge read the charges out loud. To my surprise, he was reading charges I wasn't even familiar with. He read off 'Mail fraud' and other charges. I had no clue. I looked back at my attorney, and he just nodded his head and gave me a reassuring look. I figured he would explain it to me later.

"The judge asked me how I pled and, my attorney answered for me, 'Not guilty.' Thank God, because I was in a state of confusion and physically drained. The judge asked the prosecutor what he wanted bail set at. He replied with some ridiculously high amount. Then, my attorney told the judge this was my first arrest, that I had no priors, and was not a flight risk due to my ties to the community and my three children. The judge sat in silence for a while, and I could see him writing.

"After what seemed like an eternity, he set bail at a lower amount than even my attorney had asked for. Imagine that. He then asked how I was going to pay. My attorney looked back and motioned my brother and husband to come forward. The judge looked over at them and told them the repercussions if I were to skip bail. He asked if they were still willing to post bail, and they agreed. He told them where to go to sign the papers. And with that, he banged the gavel, and said in parting, 'Good luck, young lady.' When he banged the gavel, I almost jumped out of my skin. It seemed so loud and imposing. I was still shivering.

"My attorney put his arm around me and led me to the marshals. I said, 'No, no, I'm free now.' My attorney responded, 'They have to sign you off to release you.'"

"What were you feeling then, Janie?"

"A sense of dread. Those marshals didn't give a rat's ass if I went to prison for 100 years. They delighted in making my life miserable. They were the same ones who put me on public display at McDonald's while they ate their breakfast of hash brown and biscuits."

"Was a feeling of dread something new to you? Different from excitement?"

"Yes. My head was swirling. One minute I wanted to break down and cry; the next minute I wanted to knock out someone's teeth; the next minute I wanted to laugh hysterically. It was a rollercoaster. But when the marshals finally released me, I was exhausted. My brother, husband, and attorney were waiting for me in the lobby. My brother took me by the hand and led me out the front door of the Federal Building. Once I was outside in the sunshine, I started to warm up. My brother turned to me, the sun hitting his face, and said, 'Let's go home, Bonnie. We've had enough excitement for one day.'"

"Bonnie and Clyde?" Dr. Marks said.

"Yeah, it lightened up the moment. Once I got home, I just fell into bed. But not before I took off that pink sheer nighty and put on a pair of long johns I kept tucked away for winter. I curled up, pulled the comforter up to my chin. I looked up at my ceiling and said, 'Thank You, Lord, for getting me home, and thank You for my brother and my husband.' And you know what, Dr. Marks? I think since the mania started, this was the first time I prayed or really slept".

CHAPTER 18

"**GOOD NEWS, DR. MARKS.** I'm getting out of the halfway house next week!"

"That's wonderful, Janie."

"Finally, I won't be watched twenty-four hours a day. Finally."

"It's been quite a long journey. Don't be surprised if you feel a letdown. Great changes in life, even for the better, can be difficult."

"I don't think so, not this time. After all that I've been through, I'm glad to get all this horror behind me."

"Speaking of which, last time we were talking about your arraignment. Your husband and brother came to post bail. What happened next?"

"After I was booked, my attorney and I got together every week to prepare for trial. He had pretty much talked me into the insanity defense, so it was going to be a jury trial."

"How did your family handle that?"

"Oh, shit, I don't even remember. The kids were on remote, sort of raising themselves. Mike and I were separated. Finally, the bank foreclosed on the house, and I moved in with the kids and Mike."

"Still having an affair with the druggie boyfriend?"

"Nope, that ended. But I was still manic, really manic. You could say I was at the top of my crazy game. I took up with a guy, a boy really, who was thirteen years younger. I was forty, he was twenty-seven. And while you think that might have been awkward, it wasn't. We blended well and were very compatible. And, Dr. Marks, before you judge me, he wasn't married and didn't have children."

"That's fine, but I sense a big 'but' coming."

"Well, you'd be right about that. The 'but' is that he was crazed, over the top. He scared my kids."

"Crazed how?"

"He was also manic, I think. Well, in my unprofessional opinion."

"Just for the record, Janie, everything is your unprofessional opinion."

"Except, fuck you, now that's a professional opinion."

He hesitated for a moment. It seemed as though he was going to take me on, but then he went on as though I hadn't even said that. "The crazier the better, right?"

"Exactly. So, I'm seeing him and living with Mike, the kids are on remote, my mom isn't speaking to me, I just lost my home of fifteen years, I'm on trial for my freedom, and I'm flat broke. Other than that, life was peachy."

"Feeling sarcastic today, Janie?"

"You bet your ass, Doc."

"You're entitled. Continue."

"Every week my attorney and I would meet, sometimes more than once. My trial was set for June. One day, he called and told me to come in right away, he had something interesting to show me. I rushed to his office, and he showed me a letter from the prosecutor stating they were going to send me to their own psychiatrist for evaluation. They had set up an appointment in January for a four-hour evaluation and an I.Q. test. My attorney explained this psychiatrist's job was to prove I was mentally fit. In other words, Dr. Marks, the government was going to prove I knew exactly what I was doing."

"Did you, Janie?"

"Did I what?"

"Did you know what you were doing?"

"Well, I knew it was against the law to bring in women on tourist visas who were really going to work, but the consequences didn't seem to matter. I never felt the impact of what I was doing. When I'm on my meds and thinking straight, I feel every impact of the choices I make. You think ahead, you plan ahead, you can visualize ahead. Not with mania. You live only in the moment. In your mind, you minimize all the consequences of your actions."

"Did you go see the government's psychiatrist?"

"Yep. On the morning of the visit, it was below zero outside. I got in my car, and the defroster was barely working. It was an hour drive, and I was frozen in my car seat. I got on the highway and drove as slowly as I could. I could barely see out the windshield. Frost would build up, and I would have to wait until my slow defrosters could clear it."

"When I arrived in his office, I could see he had a private practice. His office staff ushered me into a room and put me in front of a computer to take an I.Q. test. It took hours, Dr. Marks, hours. My eyes started to get crossed, I was so tired. When I finished, I was sent to lunch. Not really knowing where I was, not familiar with the city, and freezing my ass off, I just ended up sitting in his lobby thawing out and listening to my stomach rumble."

"An hour and a half later, a receptionist finally called my name and ushered me into his office. Wow, you should have seen this guy's office! It was decorated from top to bottom with expensive artifacts. He had a massive desk and two large wing-back chairs. He sat in his leather chair and was reading the results of my I.Q. test. He instructed me, with a wave of his hand, to sit down, and continued to read my results. When he finally spoke, he looked directly into my eyes and said, 'You know why you're here, don't you?'

"I thought, yes, I'm here to be debunked. But instead, I said, 'Yes, the government sent me here for an evaluation.' 'Why yes,' he said, 'that's exactly right. So, you can think clearly, can't you?' I answered, 'Well, yes, I think so.' Then he went on and on about how the I.Q. test score was above average. He asked me what I thought about that, and I just shrugged my shoulders. He threw me off kilter with some of his questions, like, 'Why do you think that you're above the law?' And he asked if I kept some of the au pairs in the garage. I told him, no, that was ridiculous. He then asked, 'Why would these young women, who have nothing to lose or gain, make-up such a lie?' I refused to answer, thinking whatever I said would be used against me.

"The psychiatrist then asked, 'Have you ever had an abortion?' I was shocked. I looked him right in the eye and asked, 'Why would you want to know that?' He replied, 'I think that if you had an abortion, you might feel guilty all the time and would assuage that guilt by taking in young au pairs and keeping them hostage in your garage.'

"Dr. Marks, that man was friggin' insane! He was the one who needed a psychiatrist. I looked around his office and saw pictures of him on vacation in Africa, in Europe, on ski trips. Someone was paying his exorbitant fees, but who the hell were these people? Here was a crazy man trying to prove I wasn't! Surely, he wasn't making all his money from testifying for the government, or was he?

"He then looked at me and asked, 'Why do you do the things you do?'

"'What things?' I asked.

"'You know,' he said, 'the illegal things you do?'

"'I didn't say I did anything illegal, did I?'

"'But you know you do,' he retorted.

"'I do?' I fired back.

"'Yes, you do. Now just admit it, and we'll be on our way. Stop playing games, miss.'

"I couldn't believe this guy. He was wearing a $5,000 suit, had a thriving practice from what I could see, but he was a snake in the grass. Wow, what a phony.

"'Now tell me,' he said, 'what makes you a criminal?'

"'Who said I was a criminal?' I answered.

"'Well, why else would you be here?' he argued back.

"'For starters, the government sent me,' I replied. 'No one said I was a criminal. I haven't been convicted. And why aren't you interested in my frame of mind?'

"'Because,' he said, 'you're a con artist.'

"Can you friggin' believe that? He had never met me before, never spent time with me, never evaluated me, but the government paid him to say shit to me like this. They thought I would break under this weasel. Not a chance. They underestimated me or overestimated him. I'm not sure which.

"I wanted to punch him, Dr. Marks, right in his friggin' face. One big punch and knock out that $10,000 worth of dental work. But, of course, I didn't, although I wanted to. To think this man took an oath to help people, and here he was pounding me into the ground, wanting me to mess up and admit to him things that—well, I don't even know what he wanted me to admit. He was awful, and I didn't even consider him a real psychiatrist. He was padding his wallet with taxpayers' money by seeing defendants, and it was his job to tear them apart. How could a real, caring psychiatrist do that?"

"Janie, it's done all the time. Most defendants who go to trial in a case like this are seen by their own psychiatrist and by one ordered by the court."

"Well, doesn't one just wash out the other's testimony? Why does the court even bother?"

"Do you think a prosecutor would allow just the defendant's psychiatrist to testify? The prosecution has to counter the defendant's mental health professionals with its own. Both sides want to win. It's the prosecutor's job to discredit your character and your psychiatrist's findings. The problem is that psychiatry is not exact medicine. You can't do an objective blood test to prove insanity like you can to prove diabetes. It's all awash with opinions, right or wrong."

"Well, I wasn't insane, just manic. And in my case, this prick of a psychiatrist was doing a good job of pushing his opinions. He had a lot of experience under his belt. Finally, the inquisition ended, and I left for home. A couple of weeks later, my attorney showed me the psychiatrist's findings. They were typical of someone testifying for the other side. He found me to be in my right mind, but he couldn't refute that the medication I was on could have influenced me somewhat. I guess he wanted to hold on to his license, so he had to address the medications I was on."

"How were your children faring at this point?"

I sighed. "I was a terrible mother during this time. I went from being June Cleaver to an unavailable, bad mom. I hurt my kids terribly, traumatized them by my lack of interest and by my actions. I'll never fully forgive myself. If I had a multiple personality disorder, I could blame it on one of my other personalities. But with mania, you're cognizant enough to come in out of the rain, but your moral compass, or what is acceptable behavior to you, is out of whack. What would have seemed bizarre to me when I wasn't manic or depressed became normal to me when I was sick. In fact, I would look at my mom, who at the time was screaming at me to shape up, as being unfair and just not understanding that I had found the real me. I made excuses to myself, explaining why I was being the kind of mom I had become. It sometimes feels that after a manic episode, or once you recover from depression, all you get done is saying 'I'm sorry' to everyone."

"Janie, do you think people with diabetes go around telling everyone they're sorry?"

"Why would they? They haven't wrecked anyone's life."

"Well, diabetes is an illness, no fault of the sick person, right?" I nodded. He continued, "Mental disorders are illnesses. I think you have events in your life you're sorry about, but I'm not sure you need to always feel guilty and to always tell everyone you're sorry. I think you're sorry; of course, you are, but how responsible were you for these actions? Think about that. Could you have prevented them? Hmm. I don't think so. You thought it was perfectly normal behavior. How about, you're just sorry they happened? Wouldn't that make more sense? And less guilt for you."

"But diabetes doesn't destroy families, Dr. Marks. Mania, depression, do. Especially, mania. Bottom line, I destroyed my family. Okay, my illness destroyed my family. But I had the illness. I then must have destroyed the family. How do I separate the illness from me? I am the illness."

I started to cry. For years, after I came down from my mania and started to feel 'normal' again, the prevailing emotion was guilt. Now, I was being given permission not to feel guilty. I went on, "Guilt is hard to give up, Dr. Marks. It's powerful, and unfortunately, there are always a lot of people who surround you and help reinforce that feeling. And on top of that, if I didn't feel guilty, then I would think I wasn't being remorseful enough. If I took myself off the hook, then it would feel as if I weren't taking my past actions seriously enough. Accepting guilt, in my eyes, proves that I have taken enough responsibility to punish myself. Do you kind of get it?"

"Oh, I get it, Janie, I get it. But I don't agree with it. Going back to the diabetic, how much should he punish himself for his disease? How many people who surround him reinforce his guilt? Just think about that, and we'll end for the day. Good session."

CHAPTER 19

"**DR. MARKS, IT WAS** spring, 1995, when we began gearing up for trial. It was a lot of work, and I had very strong apprehension. To my surprise, the prosecution offered a plea deal. They read their own psychiatric report, my past history with psychiatrists, and I think they believed there was no way they could show I wasn't mentally impaired. They probably weren't 100% sure the jury would go their way, so they offered up a deal. The deal was that they would reduce the counts down to one. And get this, I could pick the count. I was relieved they offered the deal but wasn't quite sure why. My lawyer was confident he could win me an acquittal with a jury. He was pacing back and forth in his office, his fingers underneath his suspenders, saying, 'I can win this one, Janie. I feel it in my bones. But it's up to you. You have to decide.'

"I asked him what would happen if I were found guilty. He told me that federal sentencing was completely different from the state, that while state judges have great latitude, federal judges have very little. He explained that if found guilty, the judge would add up the points that each count carried, basically open up a book and just follow the sentencing guidelines. The only latitude the judge would have would be within the range of the months or years in the guidelines. So, if the prescribed sentence was eighteen to twenty-four months, the judge could mete out a sentence anywhere between.

"I thought about that. I wasn't feeling quite as comfortable with being found not guilty as my attorney was. I kept asking myself, what do jurors know about mental disorders in the first place? And I knew the prosecutor would have every disgruntled client of mine up on the stand testifying that I seemed in my right mind when I was dealing with them.

"I asked my attorney what the prosecutor was asking for in sentencing. 'Five years,' he said, but then quickly added he was quite confident he could get it reduced. Five years! I wouldn't survive being away from my family for five years. It was like a death sentence! I then asked the million-dollar question. What if I were found guilty on all counts? He looked over at me. He stopped pacing and sat down. 'Fifteen years.'

"'Fifteen years for seven fucking nannies? No way!' I protested.

"'Oh yes, my dear, fifteen years,' he responded.

"'Screw it,' I told him, 'I'm taking the deal. I can't roll the dice on that. What if I'm found guilty? I'm doing the years, not you. No way, no damn way.'

"And with that, Dr. Marks, we struck a deal with the control-freak United States government."

"But you still had to be sentenced."

"Yes. We agreed on the one charge which carried five years max. But since we couldn't agree on a sentence, we left it to the federal judge. And judgment day came in May 1995. I have regrets about that day. For one, I brought my children to the sentencing and that was a mistake. I wish I had never exposed them to more drama. But I did, so that's that now.

"When I entered the courthouse that morning, there was a turnstile. I was carrying a huge poster board with a timeline of events, and I had to hold it up over my head to get it over the turnstile. *The Washington Post* was there outside taking pictures of me entering. The photographer snapped a picture of me going through the turnstile with the poster board over my head. The next day the picture was printed with a caption underneath, 'Janie Cochran Entering Court Trying to Hide Her Face.' *The Washington Post* got that wrong. I wasn't hiding anything. When the hearing started, the first thing the prosecutor did was run the BBC interview I did with that barracuda-woman reporter. I wouldn't even watch it. Then, they put up that damned government psychiatrist, their paid liar, and then...."

"Janie, you sound so bitter."

"Only speaking the truth, Dr. Marks. If it sounds bitter, I can't help that. I'm only giving you the facts."

"'The paid liar?' Facts?"

"Okay. Good point. Paid hypocrite."

"Much better, Janie," he said with a smile.

"I remember feeling a mixture of sadness and outrage when I read *The Baltimore Sun* about my case. Part of the article stated, 'Cochran's defense that she was driven to flout immigration law by the 'high' induced from taking the antidepressant Prozac is a pathetic attempt to evade responsibility.' Pathetic attempt? Is this how we view mental illness? 'Pathetic' is how I felt, and now I saw it in writing. Is there any wonder why people hide their mental illness from society? Because when it's brought to the forefront, papers like *The Baltimore Sun* see it as 'pathetic.'

"Years later, when I look back at what the press wrote, I see what they wrote about me as 'pathetic.' Had anyone on their staff done research into mental illness? Probably not. They just jumped to the same conclusion most in society believe, that anyone claiming to be mentally disabled or ill is just downright "pathetic" and trying to evade responsibility. It looks like the newspaper's priority was to sell more papers by inventing evil while disregarding the negative consequences to others of what it was doing.

"Many years passed since that article, but one day recently I decided to call the *Sun* and speak to someone on staff about that article. I asked the reporter what the current attitude of *The Baltimore Sun* was concerning mental illness. The reporter asked me who I was, and after I told him, he brought up the article and said, 'We have no intention of writing about you again; it would be like writing an opinion on the enactment of Social Security.'

"So, I guess he was telling me it was very old news, and he never answered my question about the current attitude of his paper concerning mental illness. Or was it now the newspaper staff's opinion that I was once again being 'pathetic?'

"The prosecutor, as predicted, put on some clients at the sentencing who said I seemed to be in my right mind, blah, blah, blah. The prosecutor strutted back and forth in front of the judge, Perry Mason style. He finally rested, but not before he asked for the maximum sentence.

"Then, it was our turn. The first thing we did was put up our psychiatrist."

"And just who was your psychiatrist, Janie? The psychiatrist who had put you on all those antidepressants?"

"Oh no, I forgot to tell you. A month before the sentencing, my psychiatrist, the one who had started the cocktail of antidepressants, asked me to go to see him, and you know what he did? The man who was supposed to be helping me fired me. He said he had read all about my problems, and he didn't think he was the doctor for me anymore. He said he would like to help me, but didn't feel it was in my best interest. And that was it. I had no one. He did recommend another doctor, but my attorney sent me to one closer to where I lived.

"So, I met this lovable Irish doctor. He went over my records and said, 'Janie, are you aware you're on the wrong medications? That you've probably been manic for a couple of years?' He explained what a manic-depressive is and said he was very sorry, but he didn't know where to go with all this. He said that if he took me off all the meds, the crash could be difficult, and this was a crucial time in my life with the sentencing hearing coming up. And yet, he stated that if he didn't do anything about it, he would be acting incompetently. In the end, he just reduced the dosage of antidepressants I was taking, but not taking me off the cocktail altogether. Being on a lower dose, I did come down from my high, but I became flatlined. And what I mean by that is…"

"I know what you mean, Janie."

"I felt nothing. I couldn't get excited or sad about a damn thing. I was either flying high on these antidepressants, or I was feeling nothing. I know that's not how they're supposed to work. So, what's the answer? Damned if I could figure it out."

"The answer is you work with your psychiatrist and find the right dosage. You don't throw the baby out with the bathwater, Janie. You might not find the right mix with antidepressants the first or second or even the third time, but you work alongside your psychiatrist until you find the right combination and dosage. Like you have now. Once you get it right, you stay compliant, like you've been doing. In most cases, a patient will feel 100% better. It's not perfect, but by trial and error, you find the solution. A lot of people start antidepressants, and if they feel 'flatlined' as you said, they immediately stop. Or, like in your case, they become manic and hide it. Some even stop taking them altogether.

"In your case, your medications weren't working because they were never tweaked. You didn't tell the psychiatrist you were flying high—or maybe you didn't even know it. But if he did know, he would have lowered your dose. Trial and error. The solution is not to stop taking them because you don't think they're working. Some patients feel better quickly on the meds, and then they stop taking them on their own. Big mistake. This drives psychiatrists nuts!"

"Dr. Marks, do you think people stop taking them because they have the problem I had with my family, that is, that they disapproved that I had to take drugs not to feel bad?"

"Certainly. There are all sorts of reasons people stop when they shouldn't. There are all sorts of reasons why people, like you, don't discuss the side effects of their medications with their psychiatrist. Psychiatrists aren't mind readers...."

"I know, I know," I said, "and they don't have crystal balls."

"The best gift patients can give themselves is to be truthful, to be patient and work out all the side effects. And, of course, it's a bonus for them to have their families involved with their treatment. Again, in your case, your husband or other family members could have gone to your psychiatrist once they noticed all the negative changes in your behavior."

"Well, that wasn't going to happen with my family. They look at anti-depressants like taking drugs bought from a corner drug dealer. Or even worse, that if you need these drugs, you're weak minded and flawed. They call antidepressants, 'nerve pills.' They say things like, 'Is so and so still taking her nerve pills? Well, she better watch out, she could get hooked.' They just don't get it."

"At the sentencing, was there testimony about the meds you were taking?"

"Yes. The Irish doctor I was telling you about did. He explained to the judge exactly what had been going on with me mentally over the last couple of years. When he got off the stand, he walked by me at the defense table and mouthed, 'Good luck.' And then the government put their psychiatrist on the stand, you know, the one with the $1,000 haircut. What could the prick say? He knew I was manic, the past records pointed that out, but he was paid by our government to debunk as much as he could. To tell you the truth, I don't even remember what he said, something along the line of 'Yes, she has had problems in the past, but she seemed to know what she was doing, blah, blah, blah.' I expected nothing less from him. He was being paid by our government to make me look like the evil one. That was his job. That's how he affords those $1,000 haircuts. He's paid to say whatever the government wants him to say. I think the judge is smart enough to see that. I don't even know why we bother with the psychiatrist thing. One washes the other out."

"You've said that before, Janie. But that's the system. And then?"

"My attorney called a few character witnesses to the stand on my behalf, and finally we put up the timeline of events. My attorney then told the judge it would not be appropriate under these circumstances to send me to prison.

"After the lunch break, I finally faced the music that had been coming my way for a very long time. In the crowd of people watching were some clients who'd lost money, and members of my family and some friends. There were also reporters there, including from my hometown paper, the one that wrote I was holding au pairs as hostages in my garage.

"The judge entered the room and asked me to stand. He began by saying he had read over everything and had given my case his full attention. Then, he looked at me from over the bench and said, 'One thing is clear, Mrs. Cochran, you have trouble with the truth. You may sit down now.' I practically fell into my chair. I could tell by his tone, he was going to send me away. He took out a book, opened it, and started talking points. He said he took away points where he felt I was legally responsible and then gave me points for things that were reported by the psychiatrist. Where I won the most points was when the judge stated that he had, key word being 'had,' to give me the most points because I had prior psychiatric treatments dating back twenty years. He was saying I didn't just dream up a mental condition in order to get a lighter sentence. The prosecutor tried to argue the point, but the judge shot him down. But the way the judge said it was like he didn't want to give me these points, but he had no other choice.

"Then, the moment of truth. When it was all over, and the dust settled, I was sentenced to eighteen months in federal prison beginning in a month, on June 1. The judge said I could self-surrender, which meant I could stay out of jail until the day the sentence began and then report to prison myself. Then it was over. The whole damn ordeal of my business and its downfall, over. I felt nothing. Not mania excitement, depression, nothing. I was kind of lightheaded.

"My kids ran up to me and started crying. My husband and my brother came up, too, and put their arms around me. It's a blur now, but I recall them saying things like, 'It's going to be all right, and you will get through it.' I just nodded my head in agreement. My friends were there, too, but I don't even remember now what they said. I was in a fog.

"I looked over at the prosecutor and my former clients. They were disappointed. The must have wanted me to get life with no chance of parole, or better yet, the electric chair. As I walked to the double doors of the courtroom, I couldn't even think of how to put one foot in front of the other. I kept thinking, I'm going to be locked away for nearly two years. Would I survive it? I didn't feel regret, I didn't feel ashamed, I didn't feel anything. Just a fog. Finally, I started to feel again. Some of that old mania I felt was rising to the surface. But also, I experienced giddy relief that it was finally over. As I left the courtroom, my hometown-paper reporter jumped in front of me and asked how I was feeling. I looked at her with disdain. That old hag had painted me as a hostage taker, and now she wanted me to comment? I looked at her and said, 'No comment.'"

"Surprised you were so civil, Janie."

"I was. Maybe I should have said more, but then I would have looked crazier than I was. Finally, *The Washington Post* reporter, David Montgomery, the poor guy who probably pulled the short straw again that day, asked now that I was sentenced to eighteen months and had three children, what was I going to do about childcare? I looked at him, and with a slight smile and a wink, said, 'I guess I'll have to bring in some au pairs.' They printed that sarcastic comment in the paper the following day. I didn't care. Up to this point, he was the only one who had gotten anything right."

"Got what right, Janie?"

"Got the facts right. And got me right, if you know what I mean. He took the time. I felt he was there to report, not to judge. He did his job and did it well. But I was surprised about the caption under my picture that day, that I was trying to hide my face. Actually, David Montgomery called the day after sentencing and apologized for the caption. He knew the truth. I wasn't trying to hide my face."

"Janie," Dr. Marks said with an accusatory tone, "do you really think you should have made that sarcastic remark after you had just been sentenced to prison time. I'm glad you kept your sense of humor, but really."

"I know that comment really pissed off my attorney. But that's not the end of it. Two weeks after the sentencing I found out I was pregnant."

"By the twenty-eight-year-old?"

"Yes. Not only was I being promiscuous, but I also didn't use protection. I immediately called my attorney and asked what to do. Dr. Marks, that son of a bitch called me a whore and said he was done with me, that I could figure it out myself. He hung up. After crying for about an hour, I called that nice woman I met the day I was arrested."

"And who was that?"

"The woman in the federal Baltimore office, the Arraignment Coordinator, the one who told the marshals to uncuff me. She gave me her card that day, so I called her and told her I was pregnant. She was very empathetic and told me to sit tight, that she would contact the judge and get back to me. And true to her word, she called me back a couple of hours later. You won't believe what she said."

"Try me, Janie; at this point, I would believe anything."

"The sentencing judge told her to tell me that he felt sorry for my predicament and he didn't want me to rush into any hasty decision. He wanted me to have another month to think about things and decide what to do. If I decided to have the baby, he said I would still have to report to the same prison, but when it got close to my delivery, I would be transferred to a federal medical center. Then, I could arrange to have a family member pick up the baby until my release. But he emphasized to her that he wasn't pressuring me into anything and to take my time and think. He also told her to tell me he was on my side during this time. Picture that. My attorney told me to fuck off, and the sentencing judge gave me emotional support. I would have liked to cut off my attorney's balls."

"Shows you, Janie, you really don't know a person until you need his support. You paid for your attorney's support, and he failed you. But the judge you thought you knew, you really didn't. Life is interesting like that."

"Well, as it turned out it didn't matter anyway. I lost the baby before I had to report to prison. I was devastated. My young boyfriend didn't take it as hard, but he was supportive. A couple of years later, he was changing a tire on the side of the road and was killed by a drunk driver. I still miss him. But I'm comforted by the thought that they're together."

"Who?"

"My young boyfriend and my child. They're together in heaven; they have one another."

CHAPTER 20

"JANIE, TELL ME ABOUT your kids. How were they holding up during all this?"

"To be honest, Dr. Marks, not that well. They were scared for me and for themselves. The world was about to change big time. Mike was gearing up to live like a bachelor and preparing to be a solo parent. I think Mike was still blaming himself for everything that went down. He told me that he kept asking himself why he didn't put a stop to the madness. And his answer was always the same. He didn't recognize the symptoms and behaviors as mental illness."

"What was your frame of mind when you reported to prison?"

"I was flat lined. All the excitement from being overmedicated and manic was basically knocked out of me with the new medications. I wasn't excited or terribly sad. It felt hard to feel anything at all. While, at one time, emotions flooded my mind, now I had to fight hard to feel anything at all. But all in all, I was mentally prepared for prison. I had lost the baby but was on good terms with my husband. We were about to be separated again, from him and from the kids. At least my mom and I were on good speaking terms again. My dad had always been on my side, but my mom and I saw things differently.

"The day I reported to Alderson, West Virginia, four hours from home, they put me in a room and told me to undress and wait for a female officer. I did and just stood there naked. When the officer came in, she did a complete cavity search of my body. And when I say a cavity search, I mean I was naked in this stark white room with heavy lighting over my head while she felt inside me with a gloved hand. An OBGYN couldn't have done a better exam. There I was, standing up and bending over, while a woman with a uniform was sticking her fingers and hands all up inside me, that is, up both pelvic openings. And while this was going on, she demanded I cough. Picture, if you will, me bending over naked, this woman feeling all inside me, while I coughed.

"I realized at this point, I had two options. One, to do exactly what they told me, and the second option, was to piss everyone off. Now, pissing everyone off doesn't mean being thrown into some small shack, into the hole like in the movies. No, pissing everyone off means you'll be scrubbing floors until they feel you've learned your lesson. Scrubbing floors on my hands and knees or doing EXACTLY what they told me to do? I went with the first option, or "Door Number One." I would do everything they told me, with some small exceptions, of course. I mean, no one does everything they're supposed to do, right, Dr. Marks?"

"I'm not surprised that you would break the rules, Janie. Continue."

"When she finished poking her fingers in me, she told me to put on a gown, and to sit there and wait for further instructions. As I waited, I took stock of my life. It really wasn't so bad. I had a good relationship with my ex, three children I loved dearly, I was on the road to recovery and I was even on good terms with my parents. They and my ex-husband were taking care of the kids while I away. Sure, Dr. Marks, I had lost everything financially. In fact, I didn't have a dollar to my name. But I was lucky that my estranged husband agreed to pay me money while we were working out the divorce. He sent me money in prison, and Dr. Marks, in prison, money is a real luxury."

"I'm sure."

"I felt warm inside. It was a nice warm. I was no longer out of control, headed for disaster. I had the love of my family. You can always rebuild financially, but you can't replace family. When they're gone, you have truly lost everything. But they weren't. I had their support, and I was feeling warm all over. The mania had subsided a lot since the Irish shrink had fine-tuned it, but it was still there somewhat. I was either feeling flatlined or somewhat excited. I sat there on that chair in the prison office, wearing my gown, waiting for the next officer to come in, and felt relief and love from my family. I prayed to God and thanked Him for that feeling. And I remembered someone once saying that God looks over drunks and fools. Thank God He saw me as the fool."

"I'm not sure it goes like that, Janie. I've never heard it said, 'He looks over fools.'"

I laughed. "Well, that's the way I remember it."

"What happened next?"

"I sat and looked out the window and observed the inmates milling about. I felt so alone. Inside prison, there is no support system from family or friends. Everyone in prison must stand alone. Finally, another officer came in and handed me a bag. It had toiletries, a comb, shampoo, deodorant, toothpaste, and a toothbrush. She motioned for me to get dressed. I followed her into a dorm with about twelve bunk beds. She told me to find one and wait for further instructions. I found a lower bunk, put away my little bag, and lay down on the bunk. I looked up, and this woman with a few missing teeth was looking down at me. 'Get up,' she said, 'that's my bunk.' I swung my legs around and sat up. I thought, oh, brother, here it comes, the inmates, the questions, the life of a prisoner!"

"Janie, before you go on, do you feel you deserved to go to prison?"

I thought, wow! What a loaded question. It was my inclination to shout back, "No! The government is screwed up." But I knew better. I had come a long way, and I knew better than to blame everything on the system. "Dr. Marks, at first I did blame the government. Then, I blamed the government and God. Then, I blamed the government, God, and me. Now, I blame no one. Yes, the government was overzealous, but I suspect they were just doing their job. And God? He didn't decide one day to strike out against me and send me to prison. And I didn't overmedicate myself and go bizarre on purpose. I've said it before, and I'll say it again, 'it was the perfect storm.' But I now know, sitting here in front of you, what I should have done. I should have fallen to my knees once *The Washington Post* reporter arrived at my door, and I should have asked God to see me through what was about to come my way. I should have never left God's side."

CHAPTER 21

"I FELT SO ISOLATED and alone, Dr. Marks. I had to adjust my life to completely new surroundings and new rules. It was all so foreign."

"A very normal reaction. It's not like you were in prison before."

"At first, I was numb. The psychiatrist I saw during my sentencing, the nice Irishman, had tweaked my medication making me less manic. I can't go as far as to say the excitement level was gone, but it was certainly lowered. I remember waking up in my bed the second day and being disoriented. I looked up at the ceiling and for a brief moment, I couldn't even remember where I was. Then, I heard the guard's whistle. I swung around and put both feet on the floor.

"It was so hot, and naturally, there was no air conditioning. It was a sweltering day in July, probably eighty degrees at seven o'clock in the morning. I was told that morning that all the newbies would be attending orientation and then given a test, that if we didn't pass, we'd have to stay in the newbie hall until we did. I began to get test anxiety. I dressed and made a beeline to the orientation room. One of the officers began to lay out the prison rules."

"What kind of rules?"

"Well, like don't bring food back to your room, don't engage in physical fights with your inmates, those sorts of things. As they were going over the commissary rules, I noticed a rather large, black woman sitting two seats away from me. She wasn't paying attention. She had her head down and was doodling on the front of her test brochure. I looked away and back at the guard who was our instructor. Finally, the guard told us to turn over the brochure and begin taking the test. We had twenty minutes. It was easy enough. When I was done, I walked my test brochure up to the front of the room and handed it in. The guard said that anyone who passed could go back to the dorm. I was happy to hear that. I was so damn hot and wanted to get my clothes off.

"Once back in the dorm, I stripped off my clothes to my bra and panties. I directed one of the electric fans toward my bunk and lay down. I had sweat rolling down my arms. Even my eyeballs were sweating. I started to cool off and drifted off to sleep. It was about eleven o'clock in the morning, and we would all be heading off to lunch soon. Not having slept well the night before, I fell into a deep sleep. Suddenly, I felt a tap on my foot. It was one of the guards."

"What did she want?"

"She said, 'Cochran, get up. They need you back in the testing room. We need you to help one of the new inmates with her test.' I was confused. I mean, how could I help anyone with that test? Anyway, I got up as I was told. As if I had a choice, right? I went over to the testing area, and there, sitting by herself at the long table, was the African American woman I had noticed earlier who had been doodling on her test brochure. The guard told me to go over to the woman and help her complete the test. I asked the guard why the woman couldn't finish the test on her own. She said the woman couldn't read.

"I walked over and sat down next to her. I introduced myself. She smiled and told me her name was Red. 'Because of the red tint in your hair?' I asked. 'Nope,' she said, 'it's 'cause I'm a redbone, black woman.' First time I had heard that before. I had no idea what she meant, and frankly, I was afraid to even ask. I told her I was hot and sleepy and wanted to get her through the test as fast as I could. I told her I would read the questions, and all she had to do was give me her answers. Seemed simple enough, huh?"

"Why do I get the feeling this is a no-good-deed-goes-unpunished story?"

"It was close to noon, and the temperature inside that room had to be close to a hundred. I sat back in my chair and started asking her the questions. At first, it was cut and dry. Then, she started to complicate things."

"How?"

"One of the questions was, 'If you were in a room and the people there were discussing committing a crime, would you: A. Tell the authorities; B. Tell no one, or C. Act like you didn't hear them?' I didn't even wait for Red's answer; I just wrote down the expected answer, 'A: Tell the authorities.'

"She said, 'Wow, Cochran, not so fast! My answer is B: Tell no one.'

"I replied, 'Come on, Red, that's not what these people want to hear. They're doing a psychological profile on us. We want to let them know we're compliant and would react the way they want. It's a choice A, Red.'

"'No, it's not, motherfucker. It's B. And let me tell you something, not only would I not tell the police, I would beat anyone's ass if they told.' She insisted, 'It's B. Put that down.'

"The next question was, 'If you saw an inmate break a rule, you would A. Turn them into the authorities; B. Tell no one, or C. Threaten the person?'

"'It's B, Cochran. Put that down.'

"'No, it's not, Red, it's A because that's what they want to hear. Get it? They don't want to hear you think criminally. It might be B in your head, but you can't tell them that.'

"'Why the fuck not?' she asked.

"'Because that's how it works, Red.'

"'Why, motherfucker? Why does it work that way?'

"'Shit, I don't know, Red. They want to see if you're willing to conform to the rules, that you're an upstanding citizen, that you wouldn't act like a criminal in here. If you don't answer the way they want you to, they'll never let you out. Quit giving me a hard time, and just answer A.'

"'Fuck you, Cochran! It's B. I ain't telling no one. And if they tell, I will kick their ass.'

"'Yes, Red, I know, but that's not what they're looking for. Oh, screw it, Red! You want B? Fine, I'll put down B. I don't care anymore.'

"And that's how it went throughout the test. I wanted to put the expected answer down, and she wanted it her way. When we were done, I turned it in. As I was walking out of the room, I thought Red's test was probably going to be the one that was answered the most truthfully. But, of course, that would not impress the prison staff favorably."

"Why not?"

"I don't know. I could just tell. Hey, I watch movies. I saw *Shawshank Redemption.*" We both started laughing. "You just know these things. Maybe it was because of what I went through, being grilled by the prick with the $1,000 haircut. What you say to guards or staff in prison can and will be used against you. Oh, and I watched a lot of *Law and Order* on TV." We both laughed again.

"Janie, did it take long to accommodate to prison life?"

"Actually, the job I was assigned helped, not because it was great, but it kept me busy. And not that it was going to get me out of my financial predicament. It paid 32 cents an hour." Dr. Marks smiled. "We were all assigned jobs. Mine was to clean the cafeteria after meals. I was given a broom, mop, bucket, and a sponge, and told to get to work. As I cleaned the floors and wiped off the tables it began to sink in how far I had come down in the work chain. Once, I was wheeling and dealing on the phone for thousands of dollars, and then I found myself cleaning floors for thirty-two cents an hour. And you know what? I found some peace cleaning those floors and toilets. All I had to do was a good job and that made everyone happy. I didn't have to be on the phone for hours trying to sell my ideas and placements with people. At the end of my work shift in prison, I took my apron off, went back to my room and lay on the bed. I was satisfied. I did a good job, and I was satisfied with a job well done, something I hadn't felt for years.

"God had done a good job putting me at the bottom. I needed to be at the bottom. I needed work where I could feel satisfied at the end of the day, and cleaning did that for me. I started to envy the lives of cleaning people all over our country. We tend to look at cleaning people as immigrants who can't find better jobs. But, really? I bet they were in a better mental space than I was when I was breaking my neck trying to make deals. I bet they went home feeling satisfied with a job well done. I had a new perspective on life and people, and I was beginning to like it. I was feeling humble, and that's where God wanted me to be.

"As time went on, I did such a good job in the cafeteria, that I was promoted to other positions in the prison. The pay stayed the same, thirty-two cents an hour, but that didn't deter me from doing a good job. In fact, I excelled at all the jobs prison gave me. I worked in the rec hall cleaning floors and toilets, followed by a routine in the weights room where I monitored the inmates who came in to use the gym equipment. It was honest work, and I didn't have to worry at the end of the day if this deal was going to go through or that deal would fail. Just clean the floors and toilets and then go back to my room. I was satisfied with the peace these jobs brought me.

"Weeks after orientation, I got assigned to my permanent room. I met a few people who seemed friendly, but mostly the inmates were closed off emotionally and to themselves. Not a lot of conversations. No one wanted to be your friend. Don't go to prison if you're looking to make friends."

"I'll keep that in mind," Dr. Marks said.

"Not that I didn't try. I met many women after orientation, but the conversations usually went like this: 'Hi, I'm Janie. I'm here for immigration fraud. Why are you here?' 'Drugs!' That was the standard answer, 'Drugs!' It seemed everyone was there on some drug-related charge. They sold them, used them, or conspired to get or sell them.

"At a given dining table, it was women sitting in a row sentenced for misappropriation of funds, bank robbery, then drug charge, drug charge, drug charge, drug charge, and so it went. It got to a point that when I met someone new, I would just automatically ask what drug charge they were there for. Did you use it, sell it, or make it? I met women who got longer sentences for drugs than some people got for murder.

"And then there were women serving time due to the 'Conspirator Law' enacted in 1985. It was usually the husband or boyfriend who was making or selling the drugs and went to jail, but if the woman benefited financially, Boom! She was doing time right along with her man, but usually with a lesser sentence. And did prison reform them? Hell, no! They were counting the days when they would get out to take up where they left off. There were a few exceptions, but they were far and few between.

"A lot of women told me they were addicted, and so they could afford to buy drugs, they resorted to dealing. But here's the million-dollar question. If they were addicted, then why were they functional in prison without drugs? Why weren't they climbing the walls without the drugs if their bodies and minds were addicted? Were they only addicted if they had access? That goes against what I've always been told, that addiction is physical and mental at the chemical level. I was always told they can't stop because they are addicted. So why in prison could they function just fine without it? I don't get it. It's not like they went to a rehab center. They went from their homes to prison. Boom! They function without drugs. So, does that mean they are only addicted when they are around it, making it only psychological?"

"That's a complex question, Janie. It depends on the drug and the circumstances."

"I was just wondering. Doesn't really matter."

"Did you find you were able to get along with your fellow inmates?"

"Most of the women went about their lives in a very unfriendly way. They didn't stop to tip their hats and say, 'Good morning.' Eyes down, keep walking. That was the norm. But if someone had it in for you, you certainly were aware of it. One woman, Sheila, seemed to have it in for me. She was a slim, black woman, maybe in her thirties. She walked like a street punk, even had her head cocked to one side when she walked. I thought she must have seen too many gangster movies when she was growing up."

"You said she had it in for you?"

"Every time she walked by me, she would mutter things under her breath, like, 'There's the yuppie girl. There's Barbie.' Or, 'There's our minivan girl.' I did my best to stay out of her way. If I saw her walking in my direction, I would turn around and walk away. I knew she could put out my lights in twenty seconds flat, and I valued my teeth."

"Were you afraid?"

"Well, yes and no. On one hand, I knew it was the grace of God keeping me from getting my ass beat, but on the other hand, I had to take the attitude of 'what will be, will be.' I couldn't emotionally afford to be on pins and needles every second. You just have to give it up and let prison life unfold as it will. One day, maybe a week after orientation, I found myself talking to Red in the smoking area, which we called the smoke shack."

"I didn't know you smoked."

"I didn't until prison. You'll do anything for entertainment in prison. You're restricted on your food intake, you're restricted with your actions, but they'll let you smoke as many cigarettes as you can get your hands on. I needed the escape; the cigarettes gave me that. I remembered Red handing me a cigarette and lighting it up outside our cell. I inhaled and immediately started coughing and coughing and coughing. Red hit me on my back, hard. I started to laugh and took another hit. You know, after months of smoking, I started to love those cigarettes. I would light up, smell that cigarette burning, and take a long drag. And guess what? It felt wonderful. I held that cigarette between my fingers and inhaled and inhaled and inhaled. Gave me something to look forward to on the inside. I could be down in the dumps but could always look forward to the smoke shack. It could be ten below and freezing, but you could find us inmates huddled together in the smoke shack sharing stories and sharing cigarettes. I loved it."

"Have you stopped now?"

"I've been thinking about it but haven't yet. I might find it very hard."

It took me a good six years after my release to finally give it up, several years after I stopped seeing Dr. Marks. I used the nicotine patch. One Saturday night, I put a patch on for the first time, and the next day I went to church. After the service, the pastor came up to me and said he noticed that I was wearing the patch. I told him I was trying to stop smoking; he said he'd say a prayer for me. Between the patch and my pastor's prayers, I never had the urge to smoke again. A patch and a prayer. I sometimes wish that I could see Dr. Marks again to tell him that I quit. But no need to go backwards; back to those thoughts of prison.

"You need to quit, Janie," he said that day.

"One day, Dr. Marks. I'm glad it helped to get me through prison. Nearly everyone smoked there. That's when we would tell each other our stories. That's when I really got to know Red. She was my age, forty-three, but boy did she look older. She was missing most of her teeth. She was raised in the streets of Detroit and was selling drugs before she was fifteen. She said if she didn't sell drugs, there would have been no way for her to make a living. At sixteen, she had a child, then another and another and another. Her mom took care of the children while Red would hit the streets selling drugs and herself. It was the only life she knew. My life was what she saw on TV. I realized she had been born into that life and knew nothing else. What comfort or advice could I give her? Nothing, that's what. I began to feel guilty talking with her."

"Why guilt, Janie?"

"Because up to this point, my life seemed like something a fairy princess would have compared to hers. I asked myself, why would I be given all the breaks and chances in life and her not so much? It all seemed so unfair."

"Mental illness is unfair. Cancer is unfair. Need I go on? Should you feel guilty every time you meet someone who has suffered in a way you haven't? In most cases when people feel guilty, they shy away in order not to feel uncomfortable. It offers more to a person who's suffering in life to try to understand the circumstances and relate in any way you can. Guilt serves no purpose."

"You're right. It was just an automatic reaction, I guess. But I think it has its usefulness. Without it, people would be hurting others a lot more. Not good! Anyway, the evening I was talking to Red outside, the night I started to smoke, we went back to our cell, and I found a guard tearing it apart and reading my letters. The guard just stood there while I protested. She would read a letter, then look up at me and smiled. I stood there stomping my feet and pulling out my hair. Red just stood there and chuckled. We just waited until the guard got bored and left.

"Red looked at me, and said, 'Cochran, now you know how I felt living in Detroit. That's how I lived my life. What with the police coming in for raids, dealers breaking in and looking for money, I've neva had no privacy. Ya lucky ya get to go home after your sentence. I've got no home to go to. Neva had it, neva will. Cochran, we live in two different worlds, and right now, Cochran, ya in my world.' She playfully slapped me on the back, which nearly knocked me down, and walked away."

"Janie, how did you feel about the guard in your room?"

"Wow! Violated, pushed around, stifled, and pissed, every negative feeling one can have. Once the guard left, I had to clean up my room and put all my papers back in order. After I put everything back, I sat down on my bunk, buried my head in my pillow and screamed. I was hot. West Virginia was so damned hot. While I was beginning to adjust, I had that young, black woman gunning for me. Prison was becoming real. I finally fell asleep that night and cursed everyone under my breath, even God. But there was one friendship, one woman who helped keep me going."

CHAPTER 22

WHILE MY SESSIONS WITH Dr. Marks were going well, I still had life going on around me. My son, Bryson, was in full swing with his love interest, Michelle. They got so serious that they announced they were getting married. They were both eighteen, but they were truly in love. My daughter, Micah, literally revamped her life by her own inner strength and found a way to enroll at a Christian college in Tennessee, and before I knew it, and with no help from me because I was so wrapped up in my own life, off she was to college. My older son, Joshua, was living on his own as well. So, one day I woke up in bed in the apartment and realized it was just my boyfriend and me. Mike and I were then separated, yet again, and headed for divorce.

And even though I had been deemed un-manic, I was still making poor choices. Like finding and living with a crack-using boyfriend. I wasn't a drug user, and then I found myself living with one as I did back in my twenties. I was such a sucker for punishment. I believed I would be his salvation. Since I couldn't save myself, I would save him. Bullshit, right?

But wait, he had a new love other than me. It was his female drug dealer. She made him an offer he just couldn't refuse, namely, "Live with me rent free and get all the crack you want." Hmmm. He probably had to mull that over for one second. Off he went and this time, it was literally just myself. I didn't like being dumped for a drug dealer, and it didn't bode well for my low self-esteem, but looking back, God did me a huge favor. If it weren't for the drug dealer taking him away, I probably would have wallowed around in that mess of a bad relationship for another couple of years. And if God had not taken him away from me first, then Satan would probably have taken us both away together, later. Thank you, God!

But soon after my crack-using boyfriend left, I started to feel like I was in withdrawal from my own addiction. I was addicted in my own way to this toxic relationship. I did all kinds of crazy things after he left. For example, wanting answers about how my ex-boyfriend felt about me—crazy I should still care, but I did—I went to a psychic. Now, that was a ridiculous move on my part. I walked into this psychic's house and sat down in her parlor on one of her folding chairs. She had a Tarot Card deck on the table, and as she shuffled through the cards, she asked me what I wanted to know.

I leaned into her as if she held all the answers to my future. On a shyness impulse, I whispered to her that I wanted to know if my ex-boyfriend still loved me and if he would return to me. She laid down a bunch of cards in front of me, and before she could answer, I jumped out of my skin when a large boom came from her huge, oak grandfather's clock. I sat back in my folding chair, and she lit a cigarette. With smoke swirling around in the air, I leaned closer to her, waiting for the answers.

After she exhaled the smoke from her cigarette into my personal space, she told me something along the line of, "The sun has to be in the seventh house of the right planet when also there is a full moon if that were to happen." I looked at her more intently and asked, "Does that mean yes or no?"

"It means," she replied, "I don't know." Shit, I had paid this psychic lady forty bucks, and she didn't know a damn thing. "But," she said loudly, which again made me jump out of my skin, "it looks like another woman is involved." Well, hell, I knew that already. She went on to say, "Love is not always meant to be."

Are you kidding me? My grandmother could have told me that, for free! "Anything else you want to know?" she asked. "Tell me your birthday and I'll do your numbers." She explained how the number thing worked, but honestly, that just confused me more.

"No, thanks," I told her and left. I've never been back to a psychic since and probably won't be seeing one again. But that shows how desperate for answers I was that I went to extreme measures. But if a psychic didn't know, no one from this earth knew. I had to heal and pray to find the answers I was seeking. And that took time, but the answers did come. And when they came, I no longer wanted or cared about being with this crack boyfriend. I was over my addiction to this relationship. I wish I could have said I was manic during these times, but I wasn't. I was just relationship-addicted, with very low self-esteem.

During these times, I found myself living at my cousin's house in one of his spare bedrooms furnished with an air mattress. I can still remember waking up one morning on that air mattress and lying there looking out the window. Gone was the crack-using boyfriend, gone was my husband of twenty-five years, gone were my beautiful home and houses, gone was my self-esteem. Had I managed to torpedo all that was important to me? But I did have Dr. Marks to talk to and help me unravel this mess.

I still had a relationship with my children, but they didn't know what to make out of me. I wasn't manic, I wasn't depressed, but I wasn't living normally either. I had gone off track and didn't know how to get back. I always thought that post-prison, everything should fall into place. I mean, I did my time, why was I still punishing myself?

I would get up in the morning at my cousin's house and just sit around all day, waiting for him to come home to have someone to talk to. I was lonely. But what I didn't realize was that I was going through a process of healing. I had to learn to live without addiction to a relationship. I had to learn to live out my days with just normalcy. It took time.

CHAPTER 23

"JANIE, YOU WERE TELLING me about that inmate, Sheila. Did she confront you at some point?"

"Interesting story, Dr. Marks. Sometimes, you never know where life leads you. This Sheila woman kept making it a point to make my life miserable. So miserable, I asked Red to be my protector. My proposition was that if Red would put out the word, she was protecting me, I would buy her commissary. Red jumped at it. You see, Sheila's friends were on the hunt for me as well. Not only did I have to avoid Sheila, but I also had to avoid her cronies. I felt I needed to protect myself, and Red was the massive force I needed. And that's how it went. I would buy commissary for Red, and she had my back. After a while, I no longer hid from Sheila or her friends. I would stride right by them and smile to myself. I knew they knew that any physical attack on me meant they would get a beat down from Red. I was actually enjoying this.

"I even got cocky. I would walk by Sheila, turn around and say, 'I'm sorry, did you say something to me?' She would kind of lunge towards me, then thought about it and backed up. One day she said, 'You won't always have Red to protect you, so you better watch out.' I just laughed; I knew I would always have Red. As long as there was a commissary, I knew I had her. Plus, I was really getting to enjoy Red. She told the most fascinating stories about life on the streets. My other

friends, as few as I had, were a mixed bag. I had some misappropria-
tions of funds, credit-union fraud, bank fraud, you know, the garden
variety of white-collar crimes. But I had one friend who was convicted
of bank robbery. She was the getaway-car person in complicity with a
bank robber. She was a tall blonde with a beautiful tattoo of a bird. Her
name was Margie.

"I asked her one day how she and her partner in crime got caught,
and she told me that when her boyfriend entered the bank and robbed
it, he came back into the car with some bags of money, and she took off.
Once they reached the beltway, one of the bags exploded and they were
both covered in purple paint. She said the windshield was so coated
with paint that they had to pull over and wipe it away. And when they
did, they were caught.

"Just hearing how the bag exploded and they were covered in paint,
I started to laugh. And once I started laughing, I couldn't stop. I guess
it was tension, I don't know, but I couldn't stop laughing. Finally, one
of the control-freak guards came into our room and told me to shut
up. Tears were rolling down my face, I was laughing so hard and loud.

"Once I composed myself, I asked Margie why in the world would
they go into a bank and rob it. I mean, apart from the obvious reason
of wanting money, why would they take such a chance? I pointed out
to her that the big money was to be gotten in white-collar crimes, not
overt crimes, and that the white-collar crimes typically get less time in
federal prison, even though they may hurt many more people than are
hurt by a blue-collar crime. She added that they were doing drugs that
day and ran out of their junk. So, after scrambling around for hours
trying to find money, on the spur of the moment, they decided to rob
the local bank. It was done without planning or even reasoning. It was
a need for drugs and a need for them immediately.

"And she was right. White-collar crimes are usually planned out and
usually with precision, meaning very premeditated, unless the person

is completely insane or manic. Bank robberies and other robberies are usually unplanned to any significant detail, and the motive behind them is related to the severe and crazed craving for drugs. They are more like crimes of passion. I understood what she was telling me."

"Janie, not all bank robberies are on the spur of the moment."

"That might be true, Dr. Marks, but in my experience, I met more women like Margie who were convicted of crimes related to drugs, usually brought about by desperate impulses and not very well thought out. Margie explained it well when she said, 'When you run out of drugs and you want more... It's all about the NOW.' She explained that your need for drugs immediately trumps your common sense and often your morality."

"But do you find *that* as an excuse to commit a crime?"

"Not at all. But it brings an understanding of why Margie and people like her commit such acts. And it actually scares me. I don't want to get in the way of someone on the hunt for drug money. They seem desperate and will do anything to get money for their need. Shit, she scared me to death. Rob a bank? Sure. Rob a person, why not? That's the mentality, and it scares me."

"It should."

"So, what do we do about it, Dr. Marks?"

"Wow! I wish I had the answer to that, Janie. Me and a million others. No answer yet, I'm afraid. We lock them up, but as you can see, that doesn't work. Letting them off without any consequences is not the answer either. Put them in rehab? Sometimes it helps, but not usually in the long run. No pat answer. It's a work in progress trying to figure it all out."

"It was two months after I entered prison. The O.J. Simpson verdict came in! Dr. Marks, what a day that was. They took all the inmates and sequestered us in our assigned buildings. We were instructed to take our seats and not to walk around or move. We were told to be quiet, and if we had any questions, they would be answered after the verdict was announced. So, I took my seat, looked around the room and noticed there had to be at least six guards surrounding all the windows and exits. They were there ready to bring order if a riot broke out. And I suspect they expected a riot if O.J. were found guilty. You could feel the tension building up in the room as we watched the proceedings on TV, the lawyers and O.J. taking their positions waiting for the verdict. You could have heard a mouse cough in that room. Everyone was silent as one of the jurors read the verdict.

"'Not guilty!' Everyone was silent for a moment, and then applause and cheers interrupted the silence. Women, mainly black women, were dancing around the room high fiving one another. The other women, mainly the white ones, including me, sat in silence. I didn't know what to do. I was in total disagreement with the verdict. I had watched the trial all summer long but didn't dare say what I was thinking.

"In the prison where I was, Dr. Marks, whites were the minority. Be that right, be that wrong, that's the way it was. People like me that day generally didn't speak up against the circumstantial majority if they thought they're going to get their ass beat. We were instructed to go back to our rooms and wait for further instructions. As the white women walked down the hallways, we would steal glances at one another and roll our eyes. And, Dr. Marks, that was not a statement about how I feel about black people. It's how I felt about O.J.'s verdict. He could have been red, purple, green, or mauve; I simply didn't believe he was innocent, and I believed that a jury of black people didn't convict him because he was a hero and was a role model for some black people. I think that made it hard for them to send him away for the rest of his life. Add to that fact that he killed his beautiful blonde wife, and thought, some, that she had it coming to her since she stole him away from his first black wife. Do I believe all black people feel that way? Absolutely not. But those jurors? Yes. I got very caught up in the trial and felt justice was not served to those people who were killed. I was mad!

"I was upset that race was a big factor in the verdict. Had O.J. been white and all the evidence that was presented been the same, he would have been found guilty, hands down. Period. I'm not a racist, believe me, but race was a factor, and it is still a factor. It probably will always be a factor as long as people look different."

"You sound angry."

"Not as much anymore. But other races have gotten away with murder because of just being of a certain color, like white. It all comes full circle. I'm sorry the families of the victims didn't get the justice they deserved for their loved ones, and I hope they find peace."

"Dr. Marks, that blizzard in 1995 hit our prison like a sledgehammer."

"I remember it quite well, Janie. I was snowed in for about three days and couldn't get into the office. Had to cancel many of my patients and reschedule them."

"The officers had the inmates out every morning before dawn to shovel sidewalks and steps. It was awful, and later, when the snow melted, it flooded the areas around the prison; and for some reason, only known to the utility companies and God, we were unable to flush our toilets and were restricted to five-minute showers. I mean the guards would call out your name and stand outside the shower with a stopwatch, and when your five minutes were up, Boom! They came in and turned the shower off. That's when we all came up with what was referred to as the TAP shower."

"I'm almost afraid to ask."

"TAP. Tits, Ass, and Pussy shower. Usually, those were the only body parts we had the time to wash. If there was any extra time left, then we washed our hair. But it was important to hit the TAP."

"How long did that go on?"

"For nearly a month. It was to conserve water, obviously. Using the bathroom and not being able to flush the toilet was like using an out-house. You would run into the bathroom and close your eyes tight, you know, not wanting to see what was in the toilet. You would close your eyes tight and just aim. Every three or four days the fire department came in and hosed the toilets out. When we saw the fire trucks come up, we would get excited because of the good-looking firemen we could flirt with, and we got clean toilets for the day. We would yell out catcalls to the firemen. Hell, some of those inmates yelled out some outright crude things to those firemen, even made me blush. It's amazing how the simplest of things, like a clean toilet, for example, can become such pleasures when you're confined. I never would have thought that someday I would find joy in the very fact that I was using a clean toilet."

"So, what was happening with the black woman who was gunning for you? Sheila?"

"Yes, Sheila. She was still giving me a hard time after the O.J. verdict. Dirty looks, dirty remarks, but I knew Red had my back. About a month after the verdict was read, I broke one of the godly rules of the prison. And you know what commandment I broke? I brought an orange back to my room. A-friggin' orange. It's funny to me now; I watch prison movies and see where there are gang rapes in prison, people being shanked, and all kinds of nasty things. And then I enter prison, expecting the worst, and I end up getting punished for bringing an orange back to my room. The system is obviously sadistic."

"Let's save the rest for next week, Janie."

"Okay," I said and left with a smile on my face.

CHAPTER 24

AFTER MY SESSION WITH Dr. Marks, I had to prepare to go to my youngest son's wedding. And to think he was all of seven when I entered prison, and there I was getting dressed to go to his wedding. I was so happy for him.

It had to be the coldest day of the year yet! It was dark outside like it wanted to snow, and you couldn't take your gloves off for fear of frostbite. It makes one long for a life in a warmer climate like Florida's. You start to ask yourself why you weren't living in a sunnier location. I parked my car at the Annapolis Courthouse where Bryson and Michelle were getting married. My oldest son Josh and I ran from my car to the courthouse, seeking warmth inside. It was every man for himself at that point.

As I ran, I slipped on a piece of ice and went flying. Luckily, I didn't fall completely down, but it gave me a scare. A scare which was enough to make me slow down and stop running. So, I did a sort of "running," but not typical running, somewhere in-between walking fast and running. Josh made it to the courthouse long before I did, but he was thirty years younger than I and in good shape.

Once inside, we rubbed our hands together and rubbed our legs. We were as stiff as popsicles. We made our way over to where Mike was sitting and plopped down on the bench beside him. A few minutes later we looked up, and I saw my handsome son walk in wearing a white shirt and a beautiful tie. Next to him was Michelle radiating. This was their day. A half-hour after they arrived, they were officially married! The reception followed at the restaurant where they had first met, and we all sat down to eat and toast the happy couple.

All my friends wanted to know why the rush to get married. Was she pregnant? No, she wasn't. She and Bryson were in love, and they wanted to do it right by getting married. They wanted to be joined together through God. And that's exactly what they did that day in the courthouse.

Micah couldn't make the wedding. She was in her third year of college in Tennessee, but she sure did call a lot that day. I tried to keep her informed of all the details, but honestly, the calls just started to get annoying. It's hard to explain what is going on when things are still going on. I finally told her I would call her at the end of the day and share everything with her.

At the time, I was still sleeping on an air mattress, but life was improving. I found peace in being alone, and I was growing both personally and spiritually. I was making friends and moving forward. My personal life was getting better and better. I wasn't dating, and that was just fine with me. I needed to be alone to process what had happened over the last couple of years. And I certainly didn't want to make another bad choice in men. I noticed that my bad choices were partly due to my low self-esteem and partly due to the fact I just didn't want to be alone. I needed to work on both. So, I did just that.

To work on my self-esteem, I started reading self-help books and practicing what they preached. I self-talked a lot, telling myself over and over that I was worthy. I felt like the guy on *Saturday Night Live* who kept looking in the mirror saying, "You're Okay, and I'm Okay, too, dammit." I stopped hanging around people who corrupted my self-esteem. This weeding-out process took over a couple of months to complete. I realized once the weeding-out process began that I had once surrounded myself with negative people who were only too happy to oblige in shooting holes in my self-esteem.

When the process was over, I was left with just a few friends, a cousin, and my children. Time to work on my loneliness. I had to start enjoying my own company and not look for others to entertain me or keep me company. This was difficult at first, but after a while, I started to realize I enjoyed spending time with just myself. I could be introspective and watch what I liked on TV, sleep when I wanted, and not have to entertain anyone else. I didn't always have to do a mood check on others. "Are you in a bad mood, honey? Is everything Okay? Do you want to talk?" I didn't have to go down that road with anyone. I got to ask myself those questions for a change.

I wasn't drinking to excess at that point and was staying compliant with my medications. I saw my psychiatrist every other month. Eventually, my self-esteem was on the rise, and I was comfortable being alone. This put me in a position where I didn't have to prowl for a boyfriend or accept what I had been accepting in males, and I actually felt good about being me. Geeze, imagine that!

Then I did something that improved my self-esteem one hundred times over. I enrolled back in college. At first, I took only classes which interested me. I was loving the discipline and the learning process the school offered.

CHAPTER 25

"SO, YOU BROKE THE cardinal rule and brought an orange back to your room. Did they put you in the hole?"

"Well, let me tell you, they were pissed off. I was called into a room with ten people. They told me I was demoted from my prison cell room to the dormitory. I had to pack up my belongings and report to ASAP. It wasn't a surprise. Other inmates told me to expect it.

"I went back to my room, packed, and went to the dorm. When I got there, I was pleasantly surprised. Back in my cell, there was a tiny window, and the room was about the size of a broom closet. It was suffocating. But in the dorm room, wow! Windows everywhere! It was large and on the first floor. This was to be my punishment? There were tons of lockers to choose from, so I picked one and started to unpack my things. A guard came in and told me to take any bunk, but not the one on the farthest right side because the other inmate had that one. I told her, 'Fine,' and kept unpacking. I was singing a Beach Boy's song, 'Fun, Fun, Fun,' out loud, loving life as it was. I was so happy to be in that dorm. 'She'll have fun, fun, fun, until her daddy takes….' Then, Bam! Someone loudly entered the room. I stopped singing.

"The locker door was blocking my view, and I heard the other inmate walk in and announce that all the lockers on the left were hers. She was barking out all of these orders, and I finally closed my locker door to look at her, and when I did, I got the surprise of my life. It was Sheila. 'What the hell you are doing here, Cochran?' she screamed."

"Were you scared?" Dr. Marks asked.

"Stunned was more like it. I looked over at her while I was slowly closing the locker door and said, 'I've been ordered to stay here for the next couple of months.'

"'What the hell did you do, Barbie, to get in here anyway? Kill Ken?' she asked, laughing. 'Don't worry why I'm here,' she added. 'Bottom line is you can't be here.'

"'Well, there's not much we can do about it, Sheila.' I knew it would be impossible to get along with her. I didn't know what else to say. She had completely caught me off guard. She then leaned in very close to me, pinned me up against the lockers, and said, 'This is my dorm room, Cochran! Don't get in my way, don't talk to me, and don't do anything in this room without my permission.'

"I could feel her breath against my face and didn't like it. I never had someone come that close to me and threaten me before. She finally moved away, and when she did, I mustered up some courage and said to her, 'I'm not asking your permission every time I do something in this room, Sheila. And if you're going to beat my ass, get it over with now and please don't knock my teeth out. I understand the prison doesn't have a very good dental plan.' I stood there looking at her as she looked me up and down.

"She finally said, 'You know I could kick your ass, don't you? I mean, it wouldn't take much effort. You look just like a white Barbie doll. Hell, I could bend you in two. But I don't want to, Cochran, because it would mean they would take away more of my good time. Can't beat your ass today. Now move.'

"I moved away from her, and to be honest, wasn't all that afraid of her anymore. Oh, that didn't mean I would be sleeping with both eyes closed, but I felt she wasn't going to be as bad as her bark. And so, we began living together. It was quiet in the dorm since we weren't speaking to each other. It was then that I saw all the sex that was going on in the prison. Sheila, as it turns out, was bisexual. She had a child from a man in New York, but she also liked women. Not me, of course, but she did like other inmates. She would sneak in women in the evenings after the lights were out, and they would go at it."

"What do you mean exactly?"

"You know, have sex. I could hear them moaning and letting out little screams. Then after an hour or so, the guest inmate would sneak out. And all this time, neither Sheila nor I would say a word to each other."

"What made Sheila think you wouldn't say anything to one of the guards?"

"Because she knew if she didn't kill me for that, one of her girlfriends would. I didn't dare say a word. Life went on this way for weeks. We would pass each other in the hallways and give one another dirty looks, then come back to the dorm at the end of the day and not say a word. You could feel the tension just building and building. My friends would ask me how it was going, and I would tell them I was just holding my own. I wasn't afraid of her, but I was certainly annoyed.

"It was about this time they called me in to see the prison psychiatrist for the first time. I was so excited about seeing someone I could talk to about my emotions, someone I could tell about my feelings, about being apart from my family and how I was coping with Sheila. I had so much to talk about. I walked into the psychiatrist's office and saw a slim, dark-headed man sitting behind a huge desk. He probably wasn't much older than me. I sat down and blurted out that I had so much to tell him I didn't know where to begin. I crossed my legs, looked up at him and said, 'I'm feeling not as manic-like as I was when I got here, but now that I'm leveling out, the guilt feelings are taking over.' I was just rambling when he interrupted me and said, 'Are you sleeping at night? Are you taking your medications as prescribed?' I told him, 'Yes,' and he wrote something on my chart. He then looked up at me and said, 'That's all. You can go now.'

"That was it? Unreal! That was it? I asked him how that could possibly be. He looked at me and said, 'I have too many inmates to talk to and not enough time to offer therapy. I'm the only psychiatrist for over a thousand inmates. I only keep up with medications. If you have a problem with your medications, then I can talk about it. And I only see the court-appointed inmates; consider yourself one of the lucky ones.' Can you believe that, Dr. Marks?"

"He could only do what he had time for, Janie. I'm not suggesting that's fair to any of the inmates, but as you say, 'It is what it is.' It's something you just had to deal with. Did you?"

"What choice did I have? Basically, he was telling me and all the other inmates that we were on our own, with no one to talk with over our feelings and emotions, except other inmates and roommates. And my roommate wasn't talking to me."

"Janie, did your family come and visit?"

"My estranged husband, Mike, would bring up the boys once a month and sometimes twice. It was a four-hour drive, and I could always count on him to bring them. Josh was around thirteen and Bryson was around five. Micah was staying with my mom in Missouri, so I didn't get to see her much at all. The whole time I was there, I saw her maybe three times. Mom and Dad lived fifteen hours away."

"Tell me about their visits."

"Bittersweet. Sweet because I got to see my children. I was so excited when the guards would call my name out and tell me I had visitors. I ran down to the visiting room. Once I got there, I was subjected to a strip search. Had to take my clothes off, stand naked, squat and cough. Then re-dress and go into the visiting area where my family was waiting.

"My two boys would immediately come up to me and give me hugs. It felt so sweet and wonderful. We would all sit down and the boys would begin talking to me at the same time. Everything felt rushed in there. Even though we had a couple of hours to visit, we just had so much to catch up on. They would tell me about school, friends, and home life, and I would listen while my eyes would tear up. We would walk around outside, and I would tell them everything was good with me, even though it wasn't. I didn't want them to know how miserable I was. My oldest, Josh, would point to other inmates and say, 'What did she do? What did that one do?' He was so fascinated and insisted on knowing their crimes.

"Mike and I would catch up on news, and then before you knew it, it was time for them to go. I felt a dread every time they stood up to say goodbye. It felt surreal. I kept thinking; this can't be happening to me. How did I get here? I was on the outside looking at myself standing there telling them goodbye. As soon as Mike said his goodbyes, my seven-year-old, Bryson, would come back for one more hug and then hold onto my leg and begin crying. I would bend over and comfort him, while Mike on one side and a guard on the other pried him away."

As I sat there with Dr. Marks and relived that time, I suddenly began to cry.

Dr. Marks handed me a Kleenex. "Get it all out, Janie. It's Okay."

"I couldn't cry there while it was happening. I couldn't let Bryson see how devastated I was. I had to be strong, and I had to keep myself strong in order not to fall apart. Did I tell you what they did to inmates who couldn't get their shit together and fell apart?

"Well, Dr. Marks, if you couldn't get hold of yourself and screamed or wouldn't comply with the guards, they'd throw you in a rubber room. The door had a small window where another inmate, who was assigned to the job, would look in on you every twenty minutes. After that, they'd make arrangements to transfer you to a mental hospital in Texas. You would stay in that rubber room for days until they could arrange for the transfer. When transfer day came, they'd come in and shackle your arms and legs together, like poultry being taken to the market, and walk you to a van where you'd be driven to the airport. You'd be escorted onto a plane, shackled, and flown to a Texas mental facility, where smoking was not allowed and you weren't allowed outside for several weeks, sometime after your evaluation.

"Now, if that didn't keep me from falling apart, nothing would. I lived in fear of that. This's why I wouldn't allow myself to feel deep down inside my soul. And remember, I was no longer excitable and manic. I was there slightly, but I was leveling out. All the emotions of guilt, love, fear, they were all there, and I couldn't take the lid off my emotions for fear of breaking down and being sent to Texas."

"Tell me more about Bryson, his reaction to having to leave you after a visit?"

"As I said, he would hold onto my leg and cry. A guard would come up to him and, with Mike's help, pry him away while pulling me away from him. Once we were separated, the guards would push me into the room next to the visiting area. Bryson could see me being pushed into the other room. He would look at me and say, 'Goodbye, Mommy.'"

"How awful for you, Janie. I'm sorry."

"And how awful for him. Once I was in the other room, I could hear his cries coming from the parking lot. While I could still hear him, the guards instructed me to undress. I had to get completely naked while listening to my child cry. Then, I had to squat and cough. I got so used to it, it was no longer humiliating. It was par for the course. But I never got used to hearing my child cry. Never. It haunts me to this day."

"I understand. I truly do."

"Janie, did you talk with any of Sheila's girlfriends she snuck in at night? Or were they not speaking to you because Sheila told them to ignore you?"

"No, I didn't speak to them, and as you commented, they didn't speak to me. Mostly, I got dirty looks from them. This went on for weeks. Then I got word from the prison staff that due to my infraction, and because the prison cell rooms were overcrowded, I would be in the dorm indefinitely. Imagine that, being with Sheila indefinitely.

"Outside of my small circle of friends, there was so much craziness going on. Women were having full-out sexual relationships with one another, and other inmates would explode over anything they thought you might be doing against them."

"Such as?"

"Well, one evening this woman, Lisa, a woman around fifty-something, asked me if I would mind dropping off her mail since I was going by the mailbox. I told her, 'No problem,' and did just what she asked. About two weeks later, I was coming out of the cafeteria, and a woman jumped me. She actually pushed me in the back, and when I turned around to see who had pushed me, there stood Lisa. She started screaming that I stole her mail. Some of my friends came along and pulled her away. I asked her what in the hell she was talking about, and she told me that none of the people she had written to said they got their mail. Therefore, Dr. Marks, I had to have stolen her mail. Ridiculous? Not to some of these women.

"While my friends were holding her back, I got up close to her and whispered to her how crazy she was. She just glared at me. I asked this crazy woman why in the world she would think I would want to steal her friggin' mail. I whispered that I had no desire to read about her mundane life. I know that wasn't nice, but I was angry. When I was done whispering in her ear, I tugged on her ear lobe and told her to never approach me again. I was turning into an aggressive person, Dr. Marks."

"I think they call that survival mode, Janie. You were put into a situation where tensions run high and people react in illogical ways. You had to become aggressive to protect yourself. I see this all the time with people who are grouped together in small surroundings and given no choices to make for themselves. Sometimes their expressions of anger are all the choices they have."

"Choices? We had no choices. Prison made us into victims. You know, halfway through my prison sentence I began to think that the DOC, Department of Corrections, should change their name to DOR, Department of Revenge."

Dr. Marks let out a slight laugh. "Why?"

"Because there were no corrections going on in prison. Most inmates were there for punishment only. Even my sentencing judge said it wasn't about rehabilitation, it was for justice. Justice? Revenge? That's how you're spending your tax dollars. I guess that's Okay with most people. I don't see any change coming."

"What do you suggest we change, Janie?"

"Stop locking up non-violent, first-time offenders for starters. Give them house arrest. Believe me, that's punishment enough. Next, make it more about rehabilitation than revenge and ask yourself if you're going to release an inmate, do you want to release a better person or do you want to damage that inmate irreparably and release him or her as a wild animal? I mean, treat the inmate as an animal, and you'll release the inmate as an animal. A very wild animal.

"Anyway, the older woman I mentioned before, Lisa? She was clearly off mentally. She would walk around with her purse clutched to her chest, muttering all day to herself. She became a target for the bullies. And in prison, there's no shortage of bullies. Where she was living, her building, there was a bathtub in the bathroom. One night, she decided to take a bath. The tub was centered in the middle of the room with walls around it that didn't go all the way to the ceiling. As she got in, several of the bullies got buckets of hot water and poured them over the walls on top of her head. She never saw it coming. She screamed out in pain and jumped out of the tub and grabbed a towel. The bullies were laughing and high fiving each other. I wasn't there but heard about it.

Those types of things went on all the time. The weak were often taken advantage of in prison.

"And what was her crime? Answering phone calls and relaying messages to her drug dealer nephew who lived with her. They got her under the conspiracy law. A first-time offense, of course, and nonviolent. And in her case, I'm not even sure she knew what her nephew was doing inside her home. She was not in her right mind. But they locked her ass up!

"And talk about the women who were there for first-time offenses, women serving time for drug offenses, money laundering, and bank fraud. If you ask me, and you haven't, it would seem better if first time offenders, nonviolent offenders were put on house arrest. This would save the taxpayers tons of money and not fracture families. The offenders could be home with ankle bracelets and still be there for their children. Furthermore, the offenders would take a kinder view of their society, and not be as likely to become antisocial. But you think that would be a piece of cake? Hell, no. They wouldn't be allowed to go shopping, drinking, and socializing… nothing great. Just stay inside, go to work, and then home. Now that's punishment. But the family stays together, and it saves the taxpayers and perhaps stops the creation of new criminals, including their own children. I wonder why it doesn't work like that."

"You think I have the answers, Janie?"

"No, but I think I do."

"Please, go ahead. I'm listening."

"They don't use house arrest because prison is a money-making enterprise. It employs many workers and makes money. If they put us on house arrest, look how many people would be put out of a job. Look how much state and federal money wouldn't be needed. Prisons and prisoners bring in money for the state and federal governments, not to mention privately operated prisons also make money. That's stupid!"

"So, you think you have this all figured out?"

"Yeah, I do. Why not put us on house arrest? We're not a threat to society. Why not keep families together? Punishment? Give me a break. They want to make money and seek revenge out of hatred. Period. And you know it!"

"No, I don't. Do some research and show me how much the states make from incarceration and how much the federal government brings in from incarcerations, and then I might believe it. Also, how many prisons are actually businesses privately owned. But I do agree that keeping families together is important, and I do believe that nonviolent offenders need to stay out of prison. So, we do agree on that."

"Want me to tell you about my lollipop moment, Dr. Marks?"

"Anything you want to tell me is fine with me, Janie."

"In life, I was concerned about a lot of things, boyfriends, friends, school, marriage, big homes, big cars, looking good to the family, fitting in with the right crowd, wearing the newest fashions, making money, you know, the things people normally treasure. But one monotonous day in prison I was walking to my job assignment, and all I could think of was a cherry Tootsie Pop. A friend, misappropriations-of-funds friend, came alongside me and asked how things were going.

"I told her I was fine and asked how she was. Then, I blurted out, 'I would do anything for a cherry Tootsie pop.' She looked at me and smiled. She reached inside her bag and pulled out a red cherry Tootsie pop and handed it to me. 'Enjoy,' she said, and then walked away to her job. I unwrapped the Tootsie pop and put it in my mouth. I was elated. All the big cars, the big houses, the vacations, the big paychecks, furniture, everything paled at that moment next to that red cherry lollipop. You see, Dr. Marks, everything in life, all the pleasures, had been reduced to that simple little lollipop. I realized then and there that nothing else mattered but simple pleasures. Simple pleasures like a red cherry lollipop and toilets that flush. So, I deduced, mind you, that happiness is a matter of perspective. I saw that everything I had been chasing was for nothing. I could still get pleasure from a simple, little lollipop. I didn't need cars, houses, vacations, and whatnot. Pleasure could be found in the simplest form. And in this case, a lollipop."

"Prison is a dangerous place. I remember one night sitting outside near the dorm room, hearing two inmates having sex. They began to argue. One of them said she was done with the other one or something along that line. One of them walked away, and later she came back swinging a sock over her head. I looked at her and couldn't understand fully what was going on, but before I knew it, she hit the other woman over the head with a sock with a metal lock inside."

"Was she dead?" Dr. Marks asked.

"Almost. She was knocked out cold. There was blood coming from her head, and she was laid out on the concrete floor. I heard a whistle blow, and several guards came running up. They cuffed the woman with the sock and took her away. It was a lovers' quarrel, but lovers' quarrels in prison end up with someone almost getting killed.

"But the violence didn't stop women from being with each other. Maybe the danger made it even more alluring. The inmates would let other women know they were free and available by wearing their pants down low, almost letting their ass crack show. It's the way young people, including my older son, are wearing their pants now. If only they knew it all started in prison and was intended for gays. Ha, go figure!

"I also noticed in prison that most people had a hair-trigger mentality. A little infraction they felt coming from another person was met with violence. No one thought shoving or pushing another person or threatening someone was out of the norm. Remember, we were all locked up in small quarters in Camp Cupcake. That's what they called the place. We were like rats there running around in a maze. And the inmates were rats themselves, Dr. Marks, you know, snitches. 'Honor among thieves?' Ha! More like 'no honor among thieves.' Any trouble I got into I was reported by another inmate. I met more inmates willing to turn you into the guards than I could shake a stick at. Now, mind you, while they were criminals on the outside, on the inside they would do anything to curry favor with the guards.

"One time I wrote a short story. That was something I got into in prison. After I wrote this one story, I wanted to share it with one of my friends, so I went to put it on her bed. Now, that was forbidden. You were not allowed to go into another inmate's cell. But no one was there, or so I thought, and I entered the cell and threw the papers onto her bed. All of a sudden, I heard a whistle blow. I looked up and saw this massive guard coming towards me. She must have weighed three hundred lbs. 'What are you doing, Cochran?' she blurted out. I was caught. I told her what I had done, and she demanded I go with her to the office. I mean, really, I'm a grown-ass forty-year-old woman, and I'm told to go to the principal's office. It's fucking stupid. And boy, do you ever give up your First-Amendment rights when you're in jail.

"Turns out, one of the inmates saw me enter the room and told the guard. That's how they do it in prison. Movies show inmates covering each other's asses. Not true. Inmates want favors from the guards. They want appreciation, admiration, you name it. They'll turn you in faster than your head can turn. You can only trust your dorm mates, room-mates, and lovers. I trusted no one. And lies? Oh, the lies the inmates will tell about you. If an inmate has it in for you, she'll tell a guard you have contraband. Then the guards come in and toss your room. Have you ever had your room tossed? They come in and tear everything apart. Everything you have put in order, every paper, drawing, picture, and pencil. They read your personal papers, throw your pillow around, your sheets, your blankets. Every personal item you have is thrown in the air. And what are they looking for? An orange? Some grapes? Maybe some candy you have tucked away? It's nonsense. There is so little humanity in the federal prisons.

"But it's not about tossing your room. It's about them, the prison staff, letting you know they have complete power over your life. And it's not just a threat, it's a reality. They have complete power over your life. They're control freaks. If they want to come into your room and toss it, they will. If they want to read your personal papers, they will. They own you."

"How did you cope with that?"

"You relinquish. You let go. No need to fight it. If you did, it would drive you insane. You just accept that you have no control over your life. You say goodbye to the old life and hello to the new life. You look at the corrections officers as authoritarians and try not to get on their radar. But I did once and in a romantic way."

"Oh, really?"

"There was a correctional officer, a man, quite good-looking. I kept flirting with him. One night, while he was making his rounds outside, he came up to me and asked me how I got there, what crime I committed, you know, that sort of thing. We got to talking. He asked if I was married and if I would ever consider having an affair with an officer.

"Oh my, I thought, here's a live one. Honestly, I thought he was the enemy. If we had been caught, he would probably blame the whole thing on me. And where would this lead anyway? And if we were to seal the deal, where would we do it? I knew he was attracted to me, but where was this thing going to land? I decided right then and there; he wasn't going to use me. I rebuffed him. I had only eighteen months to serve and wasn't going to risk everything for this guy. He took it well but told me I was passing up a lifetime opportunity. Yeah, right! On the outside, I'm not sure I would have gone for this guy. In prison, you have to weigh every action you take precisely. If I had a lot of time ahead of me, I would have taken him up on his offer in hopes of getting some favors. But with only eighteen months to serve, no way.

"In fairness, most guards were not like that guy. In the Bureau of Prisons, the federal system, most guards, or officers were required to have a bachelor's degree. Now I'm not saying that because they were college educated, they made better guards, but I am saying they were more career-oriented than state guards. Most officers in my prison were on a career path and had college degrees. They weren't going to risk their careers on having some fast and loose sex with an inmate. So, in many ways, in the federal system, inmates are safer from sexual advances. In my case, I flirted and brought it on myself. And after I rebuffed him, he took it in stride.

"Inmates have very little power over their lives. If they can gain power in any situation, they'll take it. And sex is power to inmates. If they have sex with other inmates, they begin to feel they have power over this person or that. And they begin to feel emotions. Prison stomps out pleasant or positive emotions. Sex evokes pleasant emotions."

◆ ◆ ◆

"She was seventy years old," Dr. Mark. "Can you believe that? They put a seventy-year-old woman in prison and for what? Because she answered the phone for her loved ones."

"It had to be more than that, Janie."

"Not really. They got her under the Conspiracy Act of 1985 which makes anyone guilty who conspires in a criminal act. This woman's son was selling drugs out of her basement apartment. She didn't know for sure what he was doing, but she let him live in her basement. She would get phone calls asking to speak to her son, and she'd take messages. Turns out they were his drug friends, and when the feds came down on him, they arrested her for conspiracy because she relayed messages to him. But they offered her a deal. If she would testify against her son in court, she wouldn't have to do prison time. She didn't want to send her son to prison so she refused. So, she was sent to prison under the Conspiracy Act. The fact is that they probably didn't need her to send him away. But they figured they could get more time for him if she testified. When she refused the offer, she got punished for being a mother, a seventy-year-old woman.

"Another woman I met was sent to prison for two years because her husband was dealing in meth. She knew, not like the older woman, but did nothing about it. When they arrested her husband, they arrested her too, for conspiracy. He got life, she got five years. Her whole family went down the tubes. Thank you, federal government. You are the pillar of our communities!

"One woman I met was a big-time meth dealer. She told me that if the feds had not arrested her, she would be dead. She thanked God every day she was arrested because that stopped her dealing. She was serving a ten-year sentence. She came to the weight room every day and had sex behind the treadmill with her girlfriend. I wonder if she would have felt the same way about being in prison, without her lover."

"Punishment, Dr. Marks. My judge told the prosecutor my sentence wasn't about justice, it was about punishment. Was it really? Were the women in my prison all being punished? And were their families being punished as well? Did I and the others sent to prison for punishment feel deterred from committing other crimes? In my case, yes. In many other cases, however, definitely no. It was just one more pit stop along the racetrack. Many of them have no choice, none at all.

"Take Red, for instance. After she's released, what will she return to? Will she get a job at Niemen Marcus? Get her realtor's license? I want to laugh... and cry. Red knows poverty and crime. Selling drugs was her means to an end. And prison is going to deter her? Or provide her another path? Does prison teach classes or educate the Reds of the system? Does it give them a different way of life? Hell, no. There are classes in getting your GED, but women like Red aren't encouraged to take them. They feel she's too far gone. Is there counseling available to inmates to find out what's the underlying cause of their addictions? No, of course not. Just one psychiatrist to a thousand inmates who only wants to know if you're taking your meds.

"So, what will become of Red? She'll do her time and then be released. She'll go right back to the streets of Detroit and do the same damn thing that got her in prison in the first place. And why? Because it's all she knows. It's a no-brainer. And did I feel lucky compared to the Reds? Hell, yes. I wasn't born to the streets of an inner city. I had a good dad and mom who kept me safe and educated. Lucky? Yes. Fate? Yes. And what about Red? Unlucky? I guess so. Does anyone care? I damn well hope so. Is locking up the Reds the answer? Fuck, no. But does anyone in power see that? No. They just lock them up and throw away the key. Don't even admit to their existence. Hope they fade away. But I came to love Red, and the truth was, and I hated admitting it to myself, I knew that after I was released back to the suburbs, Red would fade away for me as well."

"Every time you left the visiting room, the guards would strip you down and make you squat and cough. The idea, of course, was to see if anything fell out of your coochie that you might be smuggling into the prison. This one inmate was trying to smuggle in a diamond ring her boyfriend had given her. She had her period, and she probably figured she could put it in her pad, that when they stripped her down, they wouldn't ask her to take it off. Wrong. They did. She knew she was caught and probably knew she was going to lose her diamond ring forever. She took the pad off, folded it and threw it into the trash with the diamond ring. She then did the required squat and cough. She was given a new pad, got dressed, and left.

"But these guards were not to be fooled. They went to the trash, opened up the bloody pad, and lo and behold, they found the diamond ring. They called her down to the officer station and charged her with smuggling or some other stupid shit like that. They moved her out of her room and into a dorm. Even took away her good time. Ridiculous. Would the penal system leave its prisoners with some semblance of humanity? Of course not. We were all being robbed of who we were. I didn't like what I was turning into. I was ready to fight every day. Fight with the guards, inmates, and even God. I was one pissed-off woman. And Sheila wasn't making this situation better."

"How?"

"One night, weeks after I was put in the dorm, I was drifting off to sleep when I heard Sheila ask, 'What made you white people think you could own blacks?' I sat up in my bunk. I couldn't believe Sheila was even speaking to me, and I was trying to process what she asked me. I repeated her question back and she said, 'Yeah, that's exactly what I'm asking.'

"I turned on my night light over my head and said, 'I don't own anyone, Sheila, and I don't know anyone that does except for the Department of Corrections. If you're talking about the slave days, then I would have to say, 'I don't know. Why are you asking?'

"She answered, 'Because, Barbie, I think about my ancestors and what they went through, and I have to ask myself, what gave any white person the right to own a black person? And why did any white person think that it was Okay, Barbie, I bet if you lived back in the day, you would have thought you could have owned me.'

"'That sounds ridiculous, Sheila, but I see your point. Let's say I lived on a plantation—and, remember, I wouldn't have had TV, or read many newspapers, and I was limited to the people I had met throughout my life—and here comes my father with a group of people that looked so different from any other people that I had ever seen before. And my dad tells me they are inferior to humans and that they were meant to work on the plantation like our other livestock. I might have believed that.'

"'Yeah, Barbie, but after you met some of them and saw how human they were, you still would have gone along with that nonsense?'

"'Maybe, I don't know. If I recognized their humanity and was told not to teach them to read or write, which was the law back then, yeah, I would have questioned it. And then I probably would have asked my father what the deal was, but I'm sure back then slave owners had all the answers. I'm not sure how I would have handled it. I wish I could say I would have stood up against slavery, but then again, I'm so gullible, there's no telling. I'm just being honest. I know slave owners could be very persuasive as to why they owned slaves, even going as far as pointing out that the Bible supported it. Most of the founding fathers of our Constitution were slave owners, and to tell you the truth, Sheila, that bothers me.'

"Sheila sat up, turned on her light, and said, 'I don't understand why any white person went along with this. I have to stay strong and watch out for my race to make sure it never happens again.'

"'Oh, Sheila,' I said, 'I don't think it would ever happen here again. Not here. But I know it goes on in other places in the world. Sad. But if it makes you feel any better, all my ancestors were poor. They were working in the cotton fields right along with your ancestors. The only difference was, my ancestors, got to go to a real home at night.'

"'Well,' Sheila said to me, 'what about after slavery and even in our lifetime. Black people were thought of as inferior? Black people had to ride in the back of the bus, were not allowed to sit at restaurant counters, were not allowed to go to white schools. Did they think being black was a contagious disease whites could catch from sitting next to a black person? What the fuck, Barbie? And you're a white one.'

"'Hey, Sheila, I'm not one of anybody. That all went down before I was born, and maybe when I was a child. I will tell you this, I remember when I was around five my family taking me to the zoo in St. Louis, and there was a sign that said, 'Whites Only,' at the water fountain. I know what you're trying to say about the history of poor treatment of blacks in this country. But hell, it still goes on today. In the beginning, whites were pissed off with the blacks, now the whites and blacks are pissed off with the Mexicans. The Mexicans are pissed off with the people from India. The people from India are pissed off with the East Asians. It just has no end.'

"'And what about that sign in the zoo your pappy took you to? You didn't do a thing about it, did you, Barbie?'

"'Hell, Sheila, I was five years old, a kid. Shut up.'

"'Good night, white-ass Barbie. Talk to you tomorrow.'

"'Good night, black-ass Sheila. Talk to you tomorrow.'

"And that, Dr. Marks, is how the strangest friendship I ever had was born. I would go to my duties in the prison throughout the day, and then come back to the dorm at night and have discussions with Sheila. I actually looked forward to it every evening. We would discuss sex in prison, racism, guns, men, women. You name it. One night, Sheila asked me who Harriett Tubman was. I told her what I knew and suggested she go to the library and find a book.

"She said, 'Barbie, why don't you go and get the book for me? I don't want my girls seeing me in a punk-ass library.'

"'Oh, come on, Sheila, going into a library is not a bad thing.'

"'Then you go and get it, Barbie, if it's not such a bad thing.'

"'Oh, I see, you have to keep the badass persona going, don't you?'

"'Something like that, Barbie,' she answered, laughing.

"So, I went to the library the next evening and got the book. When I brought it to her, Sheila was sitting in the middle of the room, her girl-friend corn-rolling her hair. I gave her the book, and she started flipping through it. She would read aloud, and then she and her girlfriend, who was also black, started talking about the Underground Railroad. I sat on my bunk, kicked off my shoes, and asked them if they would have had the nerve to try and escape if they were slaves.

"'Hell, yes,' they both said.

"I laughed at both of them. 'You think it would have been that easy, huh? You know if they caught you, they would have whipped you until you passed out, or worse, cut off one of your feet. Don't you think if it were that easy, all of the slaves would have made a run for it? Hell, they were scared shitless of the 'master' and his cronies. I know I would have complied. I probably wouldn't have had the guts to go up against the establishment. Also, if I ran, where in the hell would I have gone? Plus, I would have had to leave my family behind. Think about that one, girls.'

"'I don't know,' Sheila said, 'but I would have had to do something. To just take that treatment day in and day out, no, I would have escaped.'

"'So, would I,' added her girlfriend.

"Then we talked about Harriet Tubman and how she made it possible for many slaves to escape with their families. We talked about it all night. Finally, the guard came in and told us 'lights off,' time to get to our bunks."

"Janie," Dr. Marks said, "I'm glad you and Sheila started communicating. Did that make life easier for you? Did you start to feel less tension?"

"Less tension, yes. We actually built our friendship around discussing race relations. See, there was a picture of Martin Luther King in our dormitory, and one night we started talking about him. I told Sheila I thought he was the greatest black person to ever live. She sat up in bed, turned on the light, and said she agreed. She said, 'I didn't think most whites liked him.' I told her she was crazy. Many, many whites loved and adored him. We talked about how he took on injustice and peacefully protested for black rights. And we both wondered why we didn't see more people like Martin Luther King.

"I said, 'People like Martin Luther King come along once in a lifetime.' We talked about how he saw a glimpse of heaven and foresaw his death. And during these conversations, Dr. Marks, she wasn't black, and I wasn't white. We were just two people, who, in regular life, would never have even spoken to each other much less discuss life, become friends. Sheila became my friend, a very good friend. At night we would play our cassette players. One song we played over and over was "Back in the USSR" by the Beatles. We would dance and dance and show off our dance moves. The other song we played over and over was "Give Me Shelter" by the Rolling Stones.

"One night, Shelia interrupted my dancing and said, 'You can't dance, white girl. Let me show you how it's done.' She would bust out some really impressive dance moves. I looked at her one night while she was dancing and, trying to piss her off, said, 'You blacks dance well; you have rhythm.'

"She stopped instantly, turned down the music, and said, 'You trying to piss me off?' She knew what I was doing. We both started to laugh. She knew I didn't mean it as a racist remark. I was just messing with her, or was I? I mean really, blacks do dance better than whites. Ever see most white men dance? She turned the music back up, grabbed my had, and we danced to the Beatles. I know she would have preferred different music. She was younger and more hip, but it was the only music we could get our hands on.

"One day, we decided to change bunks. That night, after we went to sleep, I felt an arm around my waist, and someone whispered in my ear, 'Hi, baby, it's me.' My head was facing the wall, and I awoke immediately. She slipped her hand between my legs and began to moan. I quickly turned over and was face to face with Sheila's girlfriend.

"'What the fuck!' she blurted out, 'what are you doing here?'

"'What the hell are you doing here?' I said.

"'I thought you were Sheila!'

"In the darkness, she couldn't see that Sheila and I had exchanged beds. In the dark, I had become a black person."

"Did that scare you?" Dr. Marks asked.

"No, not at all. I thought it was funny. After she realized I wasn't Sheila, she stood up and said, in a loud voice, 'Hey, nigger, where are you?'

"Sheila turned on the light and pulled her girlfriend to bed. We turned out the lights and tried to get back to sleep. I sat up and turned the lights back on. I was puzzled. I asked them, 'Why do black people call each other, 'nigger,' and then get incensed when white people say it? I mean, you keep the name alive, after all. You won't let the word die a natural death. Isn't it degrading even if a black person says it?'

"Sheila sat up. 'Barbie, what the hell are you talking about?'

"'I'm talking about how my kids in school hear black people use the word 'nigger' as a term of endearment. My kids know that when a white person uses it, it's like throwing daggers. They figured it out very quickly. But if I were to ask my children what the word 'kike' meant, they wouldn't even know.'

"'I don't know either,' replied Sheila's girlfriend, while Sheila shook her head that she didn't either.

"'Interesting that neither one of you know that word. It's a degrading name used against Jews. For a Jew to be called a kike is like a black person being called a nigger. But you don't hear Jews slapping each other on the back and saying to one another, 'Hey, kike, what up!' No, they knew how disgusting the word was, and they let it die, so much that a lot of people never even heard the word. Shouldn't the same happen with the word 'nigger' like the Jews treated the word 'kike'? Bottom line, let the fucking word die already.'

"'Okay, we get your point,' Sheila said, 'but we're tired; let's talk about it tomorrow.' And then we went to sleep. But I felt I made my point, don't you, Dr. Marks?"

"Yes, Janie, and a good point it is. Many words are kept alive by constant repetition. It is important to tell our children not to say certain things. People repeat what they hear. Good session, Janie. I'm afraid not only is the session over, but our time together is coming to an end soon. We have to wrap this all up. You're ready to move on with your life. I'm very proud of the progress you've made."

CHAPTER 26

DR. MARKS STARTED THE session by asking me how my personal life was going. I told him I had joined a dating site and that someday I would write a book about it (which I did, titled *Romantic Disclosures*). Dr. Marks was on board with me dating again but cautioned me to be very careful on those sites. He then wanted to get back to my prison experiences and what I learned from them. He was particularly interested in how I coped with the holidays while I was away from my family.

"I was depressed, it being Christmas and all."

"Quite understandable, Janie. How did you deal with it?"

"Christmas in prison is a day to reflect on how exactly fucked up your life is. It's a day that's supposed to be spent with family and friends, and there I was in some institution living with a bunch of criminals. I spent all day thinking about my family and why I wasn't with them. I added up all my failures and sank in a deep hole of depression. I counted the minutes waiting for the day to end.

"On Christmas Eve, Sheila and I hugged one another and talked about our families. She told me about her mom who was raising her ten-year-old child. She told me she was sorry for getting involved in selling drugs, but like Red, found very little opportunity in her life to make money. No excuse, but I did see where she was coming from. After sharing a cupcake, we went to bed, and in the middle of the night, a guard came in and put a bag by our feet. It woke both of us up, and we turned on our overhead lights. We looked at one another and then at the bags. Inside were lipsticks, perfume, shampoo, conditioner, hairbrushes, and nail polish. Sheila looked over at me and remarked, 'This must be from the Red Cross and these are our prisoner-of-war baggies.'

"I laughed and kept looking through the bag. I was delighted. I was given a gift, and it didn't matter if I wanted the nail polish or not. It was a gift. Something outside of the routine. Sheila and I spilled out the contents on my bunk, and then began the prison pastime of trading our belongings. That goes on all the time in prison. Trading and re-trading. Then, the next day came the hardest day in prison for any inmate, Christmas. After it was over, back to the routine of prison and everyday life, women having sex with each other, doing their mundane jobs, surviving. Sheila and I would sit up all night and discuss life, and the guards would look at us twenty-four hours a day. I guess it was amusing to them, like a TV soap opera."

"Where was Red then?"

"Oh, she was around. I didn't need her anymore. Sheila was now my friend. But I couldn't bear to cut Red out of her commissary. I kept buying her commissary once a month. She would come around the first of every month with her list, and I would take it to the commissary and get it filled. Red had found her niche. She would approach newbies who just entered the prison system, and she offered them the same deal that I had offered her. Some took her up on it and some didn't. But either way, she found a way to make money and exist.

"So, things went along as usual for prison, then I had a really bad night with Sheila. It was bitter cold outside, and we were freezing. Going out to smoke was a big deal. We ran outside, lit up, took a toke, threw the cigarette down, and ran back inside. That evening, Sheila was in a very bad mood. She got dressed for bed and barely spoke to me. I asked her what was wrong, and she told me to mind my own business. This was unusual because we talked about everything. Since we had become friends, she never spoke to me like that. I didn't want to get into an argument with her, so I turned off my light and went to sleep. Suddenly, Sheila sat up in her bunk, turned on the overhead light, and said the most unusual thing. 'You know, Barbie, we black people have hurtful names for white people as well.'

"'What is wrong with you, Sheila? Why are you doing this?'

"'Because I'm sick and tired of being looked at like a second-class citizen by whites.'

"'What brought this on, Sheila? What happened today?'

"'Nothing, nothing at all. I went to work in the prison factory, and my white supervisor told me that I wasn't working as hard as I should. I just know she's a racist.'

"'And you know this how? Just because she called you out on your work, she has to be a racist? Come on, Sheila, you can't actually believe that?'

"'Yes, I can, whitey. And that's just one of the names we have for ya all.'

"'Whitey? Really? Like that name hurts any white person?'

"'How about honkie, Barbie?'

"'Honkie? Are you serious? Like that hurts any white person. Sounds like you've been watching too many bad 70s TV shows as you stole it from 'Starsky and Hutch.' Honkie? Really? You'll have to do better than that.' I sat straight up in my bunk and said, 'No word black people can call white people hurts whites as much as the word 'nigger' hurts blacks. And that is just a fact, Sheila.'

"'Casper? How does it feel to be called that, Barbie?'

"'Doesn't hurt, Sheila. I'm telling you, no name you call out will hurt a white person. But I can hurt you. How about coon? How does that feel, Sheila?'

"She came over to my bunk, brought up a chair, and we sat there across from one another slinging racist remarks.

"'Powder,' she said.

"I laughed in her face. 'Porch monkey,' I replied.

"'The man!' she fired back.

"'The man? The man? I don't even know what that means. I'm a woman, not a man, and it doesn't hurt. How about spear chucker?'

"'Enough!' she shouted.

"'Nigger! Now that hurts more than anything, doesn't it, Sheila? And that about says it all. 'Nigger' hurts. And why shouldn't it? It's meant to hurt. It's vile, demeaning, and ugly. It's meant to demoralize blacks. And yet, you turn around and use it as a word of endearment to your black friends. Go figure. Let it die, Sheila, let the word die already.'

"'But don't you see, Barbie, by calling each other 'nigger' affectionately, what we black people are doing is redefining the word, and making it less hurtful? White people have given up the right to use that word.'

"I could see her point. Maybe over time, it might work. In any case, I told Sheila, disingenuously, we both had names to hurt one another, but I really didn't believe that, Dr. Marks. I don't think there is one name a non-white race can call white people that would hurt them, except one. The one name Sheila forgot about. The only name she could have called me that I would have argued with her about. The one name most, if not all, white people dread to hear from a non-white. The name that hurts us the most."

"And that name is what, Janie?"

"Racist. Call a white person a racist, and he'll react and defend himself. He will deny, defend, and argue. That name hurts us. And I learned that from a white person who called me a racist. Then it hit me; that was the name Sheila forgot to throw at me. But there are many names a white can throw at a black person and offend them with. But not so with whites."

"And why do you think that is?"

"Probably because white people, in this country anyway, were never treated as second-class citizens. The label 'racist' is undeniably and historically applicable to whites. I learned that from a very good, young friend of mine. He taught me that."

"I agree, Janie."

"Sheila and I didn't speak for a couple of days after that. Then, one evening she slapped me on the back and said, 'Let's split these cupcakes, Barbie.'

"So, we sat down and had that package of cupcakes. Things were back to normal. We just sat there eating those cupcakes, and I was glad to have my friend back. Then, a guard came in and said, 'Cochran, the psychiatrist wants to see you.'

"Sheila laughed and told me to go see the keeper of the insane asylum. I walked into the office and saw the same man I had seen the month I arrived. He was sitting behind his desk and motioned to me to sit down. I had learned by that point to comply with no complaints or questions.

"'So, Ms. Cochran,' he began, 'how is it going?' I had to think about that one, Dr. Marks. How were things going? Did he really want to hear how things were going? Or did he just want to hear me say everything was Okay, so he could rubber stamp a piece of paper and report back that he saw me and that I was functioning alright as far as he knew?"

"Is that a question for me, Janie?"

"Yeah, it's a question for you."

"Well, first off, Ms. Cochran, how would I know since I wasn't there and didn't meet him? And as I've said before, I can't read minds, and I don't have a crystal ball. But if I had to guess, I suppose he was looking to expedite things with you and wanted to put a rubber stamp on things as you said. But why don't you tell me?"

"I was thinking that this whole psychiatrist thing in prison was one big joke. I know I said that before, but this meeting just cemented it. I knew he didn't care, that he, like the others, just didn't care."

"What do you mean, 'the others?'"

"I mean that no one in prison gives a rat's ass about you, except maybe your roomie and friends, and even that sometimes isn't enough. I understand completely now why women sought out lesbian affairs. Just to have the closeness, intimacy if you will."

"Did the doctor ask you anything about how you were feeling?"

"Nope, not a thing. No problems with the meds, so we're done. I went back to the dorm, and five minutes later, another guard came in and told me I had a visitor. It was my brother, Terry. Little did I know he would be dead a year later."

"Well, that must have picked you up. You must have been excited to see him, to break up the routine. You've said how terribly bored you were. I have to agree that monotony is a kind of prison itself. Not just the fences or walls. Nothing kills the human spirit more."

"True, Dr. Marks, I was dying from boredom, and when that guard told me my brother was there it was like a bright light came on. I could see Terry through the visiting room window, but had to go through the 'looking-glass routine' first, you know, squat and cough. When they finally took me in, I ran up to him and gave him a huge hug.

"I started flooding him with everything that had happened to me. I told him about my snack infraction that landed me in the dorm, and how it was a good thing since it led to my friendship with Sheila. Then, I noticed that Terry seemed so sad. When I asked him why he told me it was hard for him to deal with seeing me in prison."

"Of course, it was hard on him, Janie. Since no one in your family had ever been in jail, it was all so foreign. It's hard for a person to see a

loved one in a situation like that and not know how to react. He probably didn't want to overreact, not wanting to alarm you. Did he know
what happened when your mother and father came with your daughter?"

"Yeah, he did. That was even worse than when Terry came. At least
Terry didn't start to hyperventilate like dad. My father just couldn't cope
with it. It was so hard watching him run out of the room. He went out
to the car and didn't come back. I wanted so badly to go after him, but,
of course, I couldn't."

"And if you had caught up to your dad, Janie, what would you have
said to him?"

"I would have told him that I wasn't miserable. I would have told
him that actually, I was feeling much better mentally than I had before
being sent there. I would have told him I was sorry for disappointing
him, and that I would see to it that nothing like this would ever happen
again. I would have told him I was sorry for letting him down. I would
have told him how much I loved him and that it wasn't his fault. He
was a good father, Dr. Marks, and a good role model. He must have
blamed himself in some way. I would have told this great man not to
worry about me, that I was stronger than he could have imagined and
that my strength came from him, and how he taught me to love the
Lord and depend on God.

"Deep down, I was still the little girl that he gave piggyback rides at
bedtime. I wanted to thank him for being the good man that he was.
He was so good to my mother and us kids. I wanted to tell him I was
blessed for having him in my life. He was the best influence I ever had.
He was the most perfect man I had ever met. But I didn't get the chance
that day. He was so disappointed he couldn't even face me."

"Don't you see that your brother was struggling with the same feelings? He probably wanted to run out of the building, too."

"Yes, you're right, of course. But Terry did stay, and we talked for
hours. The guards announced that visiting time was over and that he

had to leave. I was so sad after he left. It's funny that as kids we couldn't stand one another, but as adults, we became best friends."

As I related to Dr. Marks these glimpses of the past, I had to cope with my memories. By the time of that session, Terry had passed away. I had flashes of him in his death bed, and the incredible pain his death caused me. I struggled not to cry. I went on.

"Terry and I started to talk every week after that. I would call him and just run through my week. He would tell me how work was going and how he was coming along in his church life. The church was so important to him. Sometimes, he and I talked about Mike. Terry and Mike actually went to the same church. I was estranged from Mike then, and I threatened that I'd confront him at their church when I was released. Terry said, 'Whoa, Bonnie,' still referring to Bonnie and Clyde, 'You're not doing that. That's my church, too.'

"Oh, and there was something else that broke up the monotony. But I can't say it was interesting for long. One day, we were all standing in the hall waiting to hear the bell telling us we could go to the cafeteria. But there was no bell. We were all getting more and more hungry and more and more agitated. Why the hell were they not ringing the bell? About thirty minutes later, still no bell. Then, the guards ushered us back into our rooms. Sheila and I sat on our bunks wondering what the hell was going on. Finally, a guard entered and asked us if we knew so and so. We said we didn't Sheila looked over at me and said, 'I bet that bitch escaped, and now we're under lockdown.'

"It was close to eight pm, and I was beyond hungry. They finally rang the bell, and when all the inmates showed up in the cafeteria, the gossip was running. The woman escaped and they hadn't found her. We would be in lockdown all evening. No walks around the prison grounds, no privileges at all. After dinner, we were escorted back to our rooms.

"That broke the monotony of the daily routine, but not in a good way. None of us liked being on lockdown."

"Did they find her?"

"Not for four months. And when they did, she was in California. A truck driver picked her up, hitchhiking. He recognized her from her picture on the news and turned her into the federal marshals. She was sent back and got another five years."

CHAPTER 27

"JANIE, IT'S TIME. YOU'VE avoided talking about your husband long enough. We don't have a lot of time left, and we need to do this. You know we do. You know you do."

"I have not been avoiding it."

"Oh, no?"

"No."

"Okay, so let's go."

I hesitated for a moment. Dr. Marks was right, of course. I just didn't want to admit it. I started to talk and then stopped.

"My point exactly," he said. "No time like the present."

"Okay, Okay." I shifted around in my chair. "It was sometime in late March. I was talking to Mike on the prison phone when he told me he had a girlfriend. That just about killed me. I was upset."

"Why, Janie? Wasn't he allowed to live? You didn't want to be married anymore."

"Well, it just bothered me. He was out there living his life, and I was inside prison not living mine. If I had been on the outside, I could have coped much better. Every phone call I made to him I ended up screaming at him for having a girlfriend. He tried to reason with me, reminding me that I had dated before I went away, but there was no reasoning with me."

"Janie, I understand how you felt. You were trapped. He was on the outside like you said, and you were feeling stuck, looking at life passing you by. You probably felt like you couldn't compete with anyone while you were locked away. I'm not saying you wanted to compete, but even if you wanted to, you were unable to."

"Yes, that's exactly how I felt. I was furious, mad, hurt, even betrayed. The only thing I can say is this, there's nothing worse than getting bad news while you're locked away. You feel helpless. You can't fight back and deal with your emotions. It's like having your hands bound behind you. Where do you go to in prison to deal with the bad news? You go to your roomie, the only personal relationship you have in prison. And even though Sheila and I weren't involved sexually, we were bonded emotionally. I told her everything, shared every emotion with her. She tried to reason with me about Mike, but I wouldn't listen. She told me if I didn't back down and stop screaming at him over the phone, he would stop taking my calls, and I would be making him even closer to his new girlfriend. Her words finally sunk in, and I did stop yelling at Mike. I eventually calmed down."

"Did he respond in a more positive way?"

"Yes. He was grateful I wasn't screaming anymore. And after a while, I began to understand. But if I hadn't had Sheila to vent to every evening, I might have flirted with suicide. Do you see now, Dr. Marks, why some people become so violent in prison? There's absolutely nowhere to vent your emotions. It's not like you can go and hang out with your friends or make an appointment to see a counselor. You can't go to work, take a ride, drink some wine, or talk on the phone for hours. Everything is limited. And the whole time your emotions are building and building until they finally burst. Hopefully, they don't burst over someone's head, but they do eventually burst."

"Wasn't this close to when you were released?"

"Yes, my sentence was shortened, to thirteen months. And the rest of the time I would be serving in the halfway house. I was told in April. In May, I would be out. Sheila didn't say anything, but I knew she was upset. She was going to miss me, but she couldn't bring herself to say it. She had another two years to go on her drug charge. When she wanted to not talk about something, she would always go back to talking about race. Not that I minded. That's what made us close in the first place.

"One night, we were sitting on her bunk and started talking about the term 'African-American.' I asked her why blacks wanted to be called that? I asked shouldn't I be called a European-American since my ancestors were from Europe? 'You're right,' she said, 'I'm very happy being referred to as black. But if people want to say African American, that's alright too. Hey, if you want to be referred to as European-American, I'm happy to do that,' she said, laughing. We agreed that whether we say black, African American, or person of color, it still feels awkward for white people to describe a black person. By the way, I asked her, am I colorless? Saying someone is a 'person of color' is stupid, as so-called white people, even albinos, also have color. And there are no such thing as truly 'black' people. They're brown, light, very dark brown or shades in-between. We, as a society, have become so sensitive that we want to sound socially respectful at all times."

"How did you feel when April came around?"

"A little numb. I think I was becoming institutionalized. I was on inmate mode like everyone else. I had become used to seeing women having sex, to seeing lesbian couples. I was used to getting either no feelings from other inmates or overreactions. I started to contact some of my friends on the outside a month before my release. See, Dr. Marks, once they lock you away, your relationships on the outside start to fade. And an inmate lets them fade because she can't relate to the lives of outsiders anymore. And worse, it feels awful to hear people talk about company picnics, movies they've seen, and family get-togethers. It's emotionally safer to accept your life on the inside. The prison, the inmates and the guards are your new life. You have to let go of the outside.

"Then, a month before my release, I was preparing myself. I was called into a meeting with one of my prison facilitators and told my release date, which as it turns out, would be my birthday. He told me I would be in a halfway house in D.C. for six months. He wanted me to give them the name of the person picking me up at the prison. He told me what time that morning to be at the office, and how I would be processed out. I couldn't believe what I was hearing. 'Being processed out of prison.' Music to my ears. I've heard of processed foods. Was I like a piece of processed cheese?

"Sheila and I were already having our goodbye talks, and my brother and I were talking about how nice it would be for me to see my family again. Terry kept saying, 'Stay out of trouble, Bonnie, you have six months in a halfway house and if you mess up, they'll keep you there.' I heeded those words. I kept my nose clean and stayed out of trouble. I planned to do my hair the day before my release. I always colored it and then added highlights. So, the day before my release, I dyed it as usual. But when I highlighted it, something went horribly wrong, and it turned almost black. I was horrified. Now, to you, that's no big deal, but to me it was."

"No, Janie," Dr. Marks said, "I think it would be a big deal. You wanted everything perfect for your release. You waited for that day for thirteen long months. It was important to you."

"I ran to my bunk in tears. I no longer looked like Barbie. Sheila came in with her girlfriend and kept asking me what was wrong. I sat up, pulled off my scarf and said, 'Look, my hair is black. I'm out of highlighter and you know the rules, I can't go back to the commissary. Anyway, it's almost six, and it's closed anyway. So, tomorrow I'm going to look like a piece of shit when I'm released. Instead of enjoying what should be one of the best days of my life, all I'll be thinking about is how long it will take me to get to the store and buy what I need to fix this mess.' I sat back on my bunk and moaned. Then, Sheila said, 'What's wrong, Barbie, you think dark hair is ugly?' She laughed and patted my knee. Gloating over her logical victory over me, Sheila said she had a few errands to run, but would be back early in the evening, and we'd talk more. I was so depressed. And on top of everything else, it was my birthday. Happy Birthday to me! I chalked it up as one of the worse birthdays ever. I was away from my family and my hair was terribly messed up. It was so hard. I just rolled over and went to sleep.

"A short time later, I heard Sheila come in. She turned on the overhead light. She was wearing a hood on her head, and when she reached inside the hood, she pulled out a package. She threw it on my bunk and said, 'Happy Birthday, Barbie.' I opened the bag and inside was a box of highlights. I looked at it and then up at her. I knew what this meant. It meant that Sheila had gone around to different buildings and called in a lot of favors. It took her hours. I jumped up and hugged her tightly. She unwrapped my arms from her neck and said, 'Now, go highlight that honkie hair of yours and stop moaning. You're driving me nuts!'

"I ran into the bathroom and did just that. When I went to bed that night, I had such a sense of peace. I thanked Sheila a hundred times, and she kept telling me to shut up because she was trying to go to sleep. She wouldn't admit it, but I knew she had to call in lots and lots of markers to get that box of highlights. I lay in my bunk that night and thought of past birthdays. I had received nice, expensive gifts from my parents, from my husband, and boyfriends over the years, but this gift from Sheila was the most precious of them all. She wanted me to go home happy. All was well with the world that night. I looked up at the stars from my bunk and thanked God for bringing me this far."

"It seems to me, Janie, Sheila loved you, loved you deeply. She loved the person you were."

"And I loved her back, Dr. Marks. To think that we would not have crossed paths in our outside worlds, and even if we had, we would have prejudged one another. I would have seen her as a punk ass, and she would have perceived me as a Barbie white girl who would have judged her. But inside those prison walls, we were the same. We were united. We loved each other."

CHAPTER 28

IT WAS MY VERY last session with Dr. Marks.

He began like it was just any other hour and that there would be many more to come. "Okay, Janie, the day of your release. Tell me all about it."

"It was such a beautiful May day. Not yet that muggy hot air. It was bright and sunny with no obnoxious humidity. I had to go through being processed out. More paperwork. I was given eighteen hours to report to the halfway house. But basically, I had my freedom back. No more fences and barbed wire keeping me locked up. I woke up that morning and took a deep breath. I was already packed. I took a quick shower, threw on my clothes and make-up, and presto, I was ready. But I had to wait until a guard came to lead me down the hallways to the processing room.

"I sat on my bunk and looked around the naked, stark room. It was all metal, metal lockers, metal beds. Pictures of Martin Luther King and John Kennedy on the walls. I was looking out the window contemplating how I was going to say my goodbyes to Sheila. All of a sudden, I heard Sheila walk into the room and speak hatefully to another inmate. 'All the lockers are mine, don't bug me, and don't take my bunk. Don't talk to me unless I talk to you first, and don't even look at me if you can help it.'

"Oh boy, I thought, here we go again, Sheila breaking bad in front of the new inmate, just like she had done to me a year before. I just smiled at the inmate because I knew she, too, would probably come to love Sheila. And so, the cycle began again.

"Mike and the boys were waiting for me in the parking lot. This time, my younger boy, Bryson, wouldn't have the guards pry him lose while he was holding onto my leg. This time, I could go home with him. As I walked through the parking lot to Mike's car, I heard a voice whisper, 'Hey, Barbie, over here.' There was Sheila in the bushes. I started to laugh, but then I saw she was crying. Never had I thought I would live to see the day this tough, New York drug dealer would cry. She didn't want to come out from the bushes and get in trouble for being there, so she just said, 'Take care, and don't come back here. And don't forget me.' Sheila handed me a folded piece of paper and gave me a wink.

"'What's this?' I asked.

"'It's my damn inmate number,' she replied. 'You'll need that to put money in my prison account.'

"I took the paper. 'Really Sheila, it's come to this?' I said with a smile.

"'You bet your sweet ass, Barbie, I need the damn money, and you'll be getting me some.'

"The guard was calling me. He wanted me at the gate. I shoved the paper in my pocket and took a last look at Sheila. As I walked to the car where my husband and kids were waiting, I thought, in the end, we are who we are. If I had been expecting some long, drawn-out, tearful goodbyes with Sheila, I would have been sadly mistaken. Her giving me her account number for money did not take away from the love I felt for her. And in the end, I was the one walking to a car that would take me back to the suburbs and away from the Reds and Sheila's. Would I send her money? Sure, why not. But I knew in time, I would stop. I would be, once again, immersed in my suburban life, and Sheila would become a distant memory. And I was just as sure I would become a distant memory to her. Was Sheila going to become my great kitchen-table story?

"I handed my paperwork to a guard and walked towards my two boys standing outside the car, waiting for me. I didn't look back. I knew I would never see Sheila again. I just knew it. And I never have. That was my life on the inside. My youngest came running up to me and threw his little arms around me. I bent down and kissed the top of his head. Josh, my older son, gave me a big hug and then so did Mike. I got into the car, and we drove off. I never looked back."

"Were you elated, Janie?"

"If that describes out-of-your-mind happiness. Not like 'manic' excitement. This was pure, unadulterated happiness. Pure."

"And then?"

"We traveled about an hour when Mike pulled into a Bob Evans restaurant. I asked him what we were doing there, and he told me we were stopping for lunch. And you know the only thing I could think of?"

"What's that?"

"How could it be lunchtime since there was no bell? I hadn't eaten one meal for the past year without having heard a bell first. When we walked in, I was very pensive. I sat down and remained very quiet. The server came to take our order. I didn't know what to tell her. I had forgotten I had a choice. I looked around at the other tables and was amazed at how people were going on in a normal way. So, I thought, this is life. I had all but forgotten. I looked up at the server and told her I would take anything she wanted to bring. Josh laughed and said, 'Mom, it doesn't work like that. You have to order your own food.' He looked over at me and added, 'Better order and eat fast, or they might change their minds and come back and get you.' And as much of a joke as that was, I was fearful of that. I ordered fast and ate fast. I wanted to rush back to the car. Once in the car, I said, 'Get me the hell out of here and fast!'"

Dr. Marks laughed.

"Okay, Dr. Marks, laugh if you want, but in my state of mind, I thought they would go over the paperwork and see a mistake. I could see the National Guard throwing me in a van and taking me back."

"Janie, I'm not laughing at you. I get it. You wanted as much distance between you and the prison as you could get."

"At the end of the day, after hours in the car, Mike pulled up in front of a building in D.C. It was a nice-looking townhouse in a very trendy area. I was a little surprised they had a halfway house in such a nice place.

"It was time for me to gather my belongings one more time and go into a new situation, with new people, new attitudes, and new rules. But I was out of prison, and I held onto that thought. We went in and waited. I used Mike's cell phone to call my brother. 'Guess where I am?' He answered, 'I hope not on the lam.' I laughed and told him that I was sitting at the halfway house and could see him that coming weekend. I thought how peaceful it was talking to Terry. He always was so calm; there was serenity in his voice. Never in a rush, always joking. How did he do that?"

"Did that help you transition?"

"Oh, yes. Knowing I could see Terry made it much easier. Still, I had no idea what to expect."

"Very different rules?" Dr. Marks asked.

"Oh, yes. Even though there was more freedom, there were still all sorts of rules. The best part was that I could go out during the day, but you had to be back by eight pm. On weekends I was allowed to be gone from Friday night through Sunday night."

"Were your fellow residents different from the inmates?"

"Not really. The crimes they committed were pretty much the same. Lots of drug charges. But for some of them, the halfway house was their punishment. They hadn't been in jail. Others, of course, like me, came from prison."

I paused for a minute, waiting for Dr. Marks to say something. What more was there to say? We had pretty much talked about everything. There was an awkward silence which he did nothing to disturb. Finally, I said, "So, that's that, Dr. Marks. You've heard it all."

"Maybe I've heard your story, Janie, but I'm not so sure you've faced all of this emotionally."

"What do you want me to say?"

"Actually, at this point, it's for me to say, especially since this is our last time together. Janie, do know the difference between situational depression and clinical depression?"

I shook my head no.

Situational depression relates to an event in your life, something particular that happened, like divorce or the death of a loved one. After a while, and with counseling, it's the type of depression that goes away, you know time heals all wounds. Also, medications can sometimes help with this type of depression. But the medication is usually short-term, that is, while you are dealing with the event. Clinical depression is caused by an inborn chemical imbalance in the brain. It's not merely reactive. Usually, it's not bought on by any particular event. In your case, it could have been marijuana, but we just don't have enough evidence to come to that conclusion. Whatever the trigger, Janie, you have a chemical imbalance. That's what caused your panic attacks."

"So, what caused the imbalance?"

"Janie, I'm not sure we'll ever know the answer to that, or that it matters. What was important was that you found a psychiatrist who treated your chemical imbalance with antidepressants. Now, when these medications are used properly and with careful monitoring, they're very effective, but psychotropic drugs do have side effects. That's where things went wrong for you. When your psychiatrist added another antidepressant, Prozac, to your treatment and failed to monitor you, he did you no favor. By taking the two at the same time you developed mania. You developed manic depression, now termed bipolar disorder.

"When you were experiencing manic episodes, you experienced high highs, with no lows. You felt grandiose and pushed out other feelings like guilt and remorse. Your mania altered your reasoning process, so to you, your unusual behavior was normal. The problem was that this went untreated for many reasons. You didn't report what was going on to your psychiatrist, so he didn't know an adjustment was needed. Also, he didn't interact with your family members which would have keyed him into the problem. It's essential that family be involved with treatment.

"Then, Janie, your mania led to bad choices. Once in prison, the medications you were put on leveled you out but left you feeling flat-lined or unemotional, leaving you with a hard time feeling excitement or disappointment. Then, when you were released from prison, you were put on new medications. That's why you were beginning to feel a deeper sense of guilt. But that's healthy, Janie. It helps you feel alive again.

"Now that you're on a proper regiment and staying compliant, that's ninety percent of the battle. This is working for you. You will only get better. Take it slowly, Janie; don't push for all the feelings to come back overnight. Now, Janie, it's your turn. Tell me what you think you've learned."

I started to well up with tears. I was quiet for a bit and looked down at the floor. Finally, I looked up at him. "What I was, what I am, and what I will become will never be defined by an isolated series of events in my life. I read that somewhere. It applies, don't you think?"

"I do. You're ready to move on."

"Prison will not define me. What led to prison will not define me. My mental disorder will not define me."

"Exactly. One last thing, Janie. Let's close the loop on your children, and our work will be done."

"You know, Dr. Marks, when I returned home after prison, my personal life was holding on by a thread and there was a strange awkwardness with the kids. My two oldest had mixed feelings about me. I had turned their lives upside down, and I'm sure they didn't know if they could trust me again. Children are no different from adults who have been hurt in life. They have PTSD from the fractured relationships and are just as scared about recommitting themselves to a relationship that hurt them.

"I let them deal with me the way they were comfortable with. They wanted emotional space. I knew I had to prove myself to them, and in time I did just that. It wasn't easy. I had to allow them to hate me. That hurt me to my core, especially since I knew I had caused it. Allowing someone to hate me and not trust me is the hardest thing I've ever done. You want to constantly bug them and tell them how much you have changed and beg them to give you another chance. But children are smarter than adults. They go with their instincts and they have no hidden agenda. They just want to be loved without being betrayed and hurt. It took time for them to trust me, and to this day I'm not sure the trust is fully there. I believe they will always have their guard up about me. But the hate is gone, and it's been replaced with love. I had to let them come to me when they were ready, and I had to work hard to prove myself. Hard work, indeed. I never threw in the towel with them. They wanted me to prove myself, and I did. It took years and years. But, oh, were they worth it! Sweet Lord, they were worth it!"

"You survived, Janie, you survived. Do you want to know why? Because you finally knew you had to help yourself. You kept your appointments with your doctors. You were compliant in taking your medications. You were strong. You finally admitted you had a problem and took it seriously. You took care of yourself. That took strength, Janie, great strength."

"My brother would have been so proud of me."

Dr. Marks smiled. "Janie, I think your brother was always proud of you, but since you were never proud of yourself, you failed to see that." He stopped for a second. I almost thought I saw a tear in his eye. "Janie," he continued, "I'm proud of you, too."

I broke down and cried. I hadn't cried like that since I was a child. It was finally behind me. I cried for my brother. I cried for my kids and what I put them through.

Dr. Marks stood up and did something he had never done before. He held me. I cried on his shoulder, his strong, powerful shoulder. I thanked him for bringing me through this journey.

He said, "Bonnie, I couldn't have done it without you," referring, of course, to what my brother had said to me on the courthouse steps. "Janie, how many psychiatrists does it take to change YOUR light bulb?"

I smiled, remembering that joke that I had told him in one of our first sessions. I looked up at him and asked, "How many?"

He put his hand on my shoulder, leaned into me and said in a low voice, "None. You changed it yourself."

I never saw Dr. Marks again. Life has its times when you have to move on.

CHAPTER 29

SEVERAL YEARS AFTER I stopped seeing Dr. Marks, I started to feel terribly anxious, and it just wouldn't go away. At the time, I had a job and was living in a townhouse. There was nothing unusual going on in my life, and I wasn't dating. I was compliant with my medications and seeing my new psychiatrist regularly. But one particular day I just started feeling horrible anxiety. It kept getting worse, and I had no idea why. I was terribly confused. I couldn't sleep and lost my appetite. My psychiatrist didn't know what was causing it, so she suggested I admit myself to a psychiatric facility.

As my son Bryson drove me there, I felt lost. I had survived so much, prison, losing my family, rebuilding my family, rebuilding my finances. I was forging new friendships only to lose them all over again because I was losing my mind. I had never felt so defeated.

After I was admitted to the hospital, it took a full day for me to see the psychiatrist. He reassured me he could readjust my medications to make me feel whole again. I didn't believe a word he said. I wasn't suicidal, but I did feel hopeless. I saw my future as spending the rest of my life in some psychiatric hospital until the day I died. I felt that if the medications failed me, as was the case then, what hope did I have?

Nothing mattered to me anymore. I loved my family but saw no future growing old with them. If someone had come into my hospital room and told me that I had just won a million-dollar lottery, it wouldn't have mattered. What joy could I feel if I couldn't think straight? My mind was taking a one-way ride to insanity, and I was in the passenger seat watching it unfold.

As the days went by, the new medication that the hospital doctor prescribed started to have a positive effect. I began to get my appetite back. I started to feel hopeful about life. I began to feel again! After a couple of days, the doctor began to see my progress and told me I could go home. My elder son, Josh, came to pick me up, and together we sat in the therapist's room as the therapist explained to Josh what to watch out for. I didn't want to hear anything about a setback. I knew I was what they now call bipolar, but I still called it manic depression, and even though I didn't want to admit it, I knew I could have setbacks. But that day, all I wanted was to leave that place.

When I got home, I sat on the couch and took an inventory of my belongings. I had my doll collection which was displayed throughout my house. I had the antiques I was so proud of, and my matching chairs, ottomans, and pillows. I had the china I had collected from my marriage, tons of clothes, designer handbags, shoes, expensive make-up, and all the collectible items I had gathered throughout the years. I just sat there alone and stared at them. I didn't care what happened to any of those damned things. Someone could have come over and moved everything out, and I wouldn't have blinked an eye.

It took having lost the most valuable thing a person has, her mind, to realize that nothing else truly matters in the world. I used to think the worst thing you could lose was your freedom. But that pales next to losing your mind. Take away your ability to think and feel, then you might as well not be alive. And to have come back from the brink of mental death, I felt a sense of freedom from material belongings. I could live without them, but how could I live without my mind? I had lost everything financially when I went to prison, but I rebuilt. But if you can't think straight, there is no rebuilding. There is nothing then.

I put my head back on the couch and said a silent prayer to God, thanking Him for rescuing my mind and giving me life again. I promised Him I would never make money or material things as high a priority as I did before. Antiques were merely wood and metal. I was flesh and bones. I had a soul. My mental breakdown had made me enlightened, and that was a good thing. I wasn't Gandhi or Confucius, but I was no longer the person I had been. I finally figured out my priorities and what in life brought me joy. And I finally figured out why I stayed in bad relationships.

I came to realize that being in a relationship can sometimes be an addiction, much like heroin. That first high you get in a relationship is embedded in your brain. I realized that I kept chasing that high, staying in bad relationships. I settled for bad times, poor treatment, but it was not in the name of love. It was in the name of addiction.

It's been over ten years since I was in that psychiatric hospital. I have yet to have another setback. I've grown personally and spiritually. To help my self-esteem, I enrolled in more college classes, earning two certificates, one in "Addiction Counseling" and the other in "Mental Health First Aid." I wrote a book, titled "Romantic Disclosures," chronicling the dates I made from the Internet. These things helped lift me from what I was.

I socialize often and have many friends, men, and women. I have not remarried, but I do like to date. Since my self-esteem is so much higher, I won't just settle for anyone. I enjoy dinners with friends and good conversations over a bottle of wine. I like shopping and spending hours with my grandchildren.

Despite that I was a terrible role model, my children went on to become successful. My daughter earned her Master's in Social Work. Joshua works for a huge cable show, and Bryson works and takes care of his family and two beautiful daughters. My daughter-in-law, one of the smarter women I've known, works part-time for her Catholic parish as a social media director, but still has the time to manage her children, her husband, and the household. My ex-husband, Mike, is still strong in his Christian faith, remarried to a wonderful woman. Together, they sing in the choir and volunteer at their local church. Mike and I remain good friends to this day.

It was a long road to get where I am now. I'm still taking medications to control my panic attacks, mania, and depression. I see my psychiatrist when I'm supposed to. There are still days I feel sorry for myself for having this disorder and curse the fact I have to take meds, but mostly I'm grateful I live in a time where we have such things to maintain mental health. I'm grateful that I learned to enjoy the simple pleasures of life, and that I no longer need the bigger and better of everything. I had that, and then I lost it all. Looking back, it meant nothing.

Epilogue:
Reflections on Prison

WHEN I THINK BACK about prison, I think a lot about Red. I quickly forgot my feelings for her as she predicted I would. I was thrown back into a society that didn't recognize the Reds of this world. I often wonder where she ended up, and I suspect it was right back in prison. Not because she's a bad person, but rather because there was no avenue for her other than drugs. Where does a middle-aged woman raised in the hood, with missing teeth, no education, and a felony record, go from there?

I had a blessing upon blessing heaped on me compared with Red. I had a husband with a good salary helping me to rebuild, a nice home, a nice income, and family support. I had many avenues to choose from. But where did I go from prison? Prison made me lazy and scared, and it murdered my self-esteem. I was scared to start a new venture fearing I would be thrown back into prison for any mistake I made. Not rational thinking, but I was experiencing a bit of PTSD.

After prison, I was a bit lazy. I wasn't eager to jump back into the work world and start taking orders again. I think prison made me feel somewhat of a burnout, someone who just wanted to coast through life. Was I a better person because of prison? No. Did prison help shape me into a more productive citizen for society? No. It just made me feel lazy and scared.

Then, I reflect on the cost to the taxpayers for my incarceration. Based on statistics, it cost the Federal government an average of $24,864 in 1995 to incarcerate me for thirteen months[1]; another $13,468 to house me in a halfway house; another $8,640 to pay for my counseling upon release from prison; and $16,425 for my medications for approximately two years. That totals $63,400 for approximately two years. An alternative to that?

An alternative for me and other inmates convicted of nonviolent crimes would be house arrest, costing the government almost nothing. We would be ordered to work daily and return home with an ankle bracelet to monitor us. We would be productive citizens of society, be allowed to keep families together, and would be kept from becoming complacent and lazy. While working, we could have earned the money to pay court costs, and in many cases, restitution. I don't know, just a thought. What do I know, right?

But one thing for sure, it would certainly save the taxpayers a ton of money or allow the taxpayers a chance to allocate that money to much more worthy causes. Violent criminals need to be imprisoned and guarded. Nonviolent criminals, not so much, is my thought. But it's the taxpayers call.

The most important things of all are God, family, and friends. Less is more in life. And, of course, I appreciate that bottle of wine and have titillating conversations where no one agrees with anyone.

The biggest lesson I've learned from all this, that it's never, ever, too late for anyone to start over again. Mental breakdowns, prison, and still more mental breakdowns, I've always managed to rebuild. And one thing is for sure, if I could do it, so can anyone, and I mean that from the bottom of my heart and soul.

---

1   Justice Department, U.S. Government, "Federal Prison System Operating Cost Per Inmate." https://www.justice.gov/archive/jmd/1975_2002/2002/html/page117-119.htm.

Now, let me take a moment to discuss who needs to come out of the closet. I'm talking about the mentally ill, anyone with a mental disorder. "Mentally ill" sounds very harsh and conjures up images of someone stumbling down the psychiatric ward with drool dripping from his mouth. But that is a mere stereotype. If there is something wrong with your brain chemistry, there is so much that can be done. No one has to drool in a psychiatric ward.

Today, treatment means taking medications and seeing a therapist. But there's a huge problem. Do the mentally ill talk about their illnesses? No. And why? Because of stigma and the perception of being judged negatively. Most of society does not understand mental illness and quick to judge those who suffer. "It's not the norm," many say. A person with mental illness is frequently viewed as weird or faking it or someone who needs to get with the program and pull herself up and get back to the business of living.

Society does accept that schizophrenia is a disease, and a real one, because there is no denying that there is something wrong with a person who hallucinates and doesn't comprehend reality. But is society accepting of depression? Or mania? Or obsessive-compulsive disorder, just to name a few? Many view depression as "having the blues," but it's a far cry from just being sad. It's a debilitating disorder that can lead to suicide. Mania can ruin lives and the lives of others. Obsessive-compulsive individuals have the highest rate of suicide, ranking after depression. And panic attacks, or acute anxiety, can sometimes lead to agoraphobia, the irrational fear of leaving your home or being alone while outdoors. Most people who have panic attacks live in constant fear of the next one. The disorder terrorizes its victims. Moreover, it's hereditary, so there's also the risk of passing it on.

So, where do people go to talk about their maladies? Their friends? I don't think so. Some so-called friends are the first to judge. And I shouldn't imply that all friends judge out of hand, but many do. They leap to conclusions and make judgments.

Most people keep it to themselves and confide to few, and this can lead to low self-esteem and self-loathing, and sometimes even right down the path to suicide. Mental illness is the illness with "shame" attached to it. It comes with a big social stigma.[2][3] How pitiful is that? Should I be ashamed of something that is happening in my brain that I have no control over? Shameful because society doesn't understand it? Don't embarrass the family, right? People will talk about you if you admit to mental illness, so keep it under wraps. No one needs to know. It's your business. I've heard it all.

Antidepressants are for the weak minded, or so I'm told. People rely on too many pills and other medications. What if I said that to a diabetic? What if I told a diabetic that he was weak-minded and relied on too much insulin and that all he needed to do was pray his disease away, to pull himself up by his bootstraps, and thus get on with life? I would sound insensitive and crazy, right? But, hey, that's what I've been told all my life about my mental illness, and no one blinked an eye.

Being gay is no longer something many people feel compelled to hide. Why should people who are mentally ill be any different? It's ignorance that keeps society from understanding mental illness. Complete and utter ignorance. People who don't understand mental illness don't talk about it. And people with mental illness, won't talk about it.

I would like to see all with mental disorders shout from the rooftops that they didn't cause their illnesses. They are not defined by their illnesses. Do we judge people for their heart problems? Diabetes? Kidney problems? No, we accept that their illnesses are no fault of

---

2   Graham C.L. Davey, "Mental Health and Stigma," *Psychology Today,* August 20, 2013. https://www.psychologytoday.com/blog/why-we-worry/201308/mental-health-stigma.

3   Patrick W. Corrigan and Amy C. Watson, "Understanding the Impact of Stigma on People with Mental Illness," *World Psychiatry* 1, no. 1 (2002): 16-20.

their own. But we are quick to judge those with mental illness as if they were the cause. Ignorance. Ignorance I'm used to seeing in people around me.

A friend of mine once told me that he told his coworker about my mental disorder, and the coworker looked over at my friend and said, "You better run, she's a mess." Not only is this an utterly ignorant statement, but let me turn this around. What if my friend told his coworker that I had cancer? Would this coworker turn to my friend and say, "You better run. She's a mess." No! Because the coworker would not want to seem insensitive to a disease we as a society are used to dealing with and viewing with kindness and empathy.

Is my illness less real than cancer? Do the mentally ill or chemically imbalanced not deserve kindness and empathy and understanding? It's become acceptable in our society to make these types of insensitive and ignorant statements, like my friend's coworker. Do I blame him? Yes, indeed, but I also blame a society that does not stand up for the mentally ill. Mental illness, for a very long time, has had no voice. I want to change that. In fact, so ingrained is blaming the mentally ill for their behavior that our justice system typically disregards mental illness as a mitigating factor in sentencing criminals.[4] It is alarming that 15% of men and 30% of women in jail have severe mental health problems.[5] As you can see, nearly one in three women that end up in jail have serious mental health issues. In effect, isn't the court system punishing many people, especially women, for being mentally ill? Is mental illness a crime? Even once the convicted person is in prison, the system turns a blind eye to mental illness and

4 Derek Denckla and Greg Berman, "Rethinking the Revolving Door: A LoOkay at Mental Illness in the Courts," *Center for Court Innovation*, 2001. http://www.courtinnovation.org/pdf/mental_health.pdf

5 National Alliance on Mental Illness (NAMI), "Jailing People with Mental Illness," https://www.nami.org/Learn-More/Public-Policy/Jailing-People-with-Mental-Illness, accessed August 25, 2017.

its implications. Prisoners who attempt suicide are routinely punished for attempting suicide.[6]

I admit I did have to take a big breath the moment this book became available. I knew judgment and stares were right around the corner. But I came out of the closet, and this is where I intend to stay. If you are suffering from mental illness, I say be strong, friend, stand tall and come out of that closet. I will support you and so will anyone who is properly educated. Hold your head up! Don't apologize for something you have no control over, and don't hang your head in shame. Stay strong and millions will follow you!

Do I sound angry? Damn right, I am. I'm tired of feeling shameful over an illness I can't control. I'm tired of apologizing to society for being sick. I'm tired of hiding and not talking about my illness while listening to someone else go on and on about her knee surgery. I'm tired of feeling ashamed, and I'm tired of feeling as if my illness is my fault.

Please come out of the closet, and I, and others like me, will be there supporting you the entire way. It's our time!

In closing, I just want to say, if you have a mental illness, be kind to yourself. And if you have a loved one or a friend, a coworker, or a neighbor who is suffering from mental illness, be kind to them as well. It's not their fault they are sick. Love them and help them to love themselves.

6 Andrew Cohen, "Should Mentally Ill Federal Prisoners Be Punished for Suicide Attempts?" *The Atlantic*, April 1, 2013. https://www.theatlantic.com/national/archive/2013/04/should-mentally-ill-federal-prisoners-be-punished-for-suicide-attempts/274313/ .

CPSIA information can be obtained
at www.ICGtesting.com
Printed in the USA
FFHW020252160819
54347486-60031FF